"Dixon's grasp on dialogue and prose is quite amazing . . . his voice is needed, and his timing is right on the mark."

—*Northwest Gay and Lesbian Reader*

"Large parts of *Vanishing Rooms* are written with lyricism so perfect that any distinction between poetry and prose is beside the point."

—*Outweek*

"POIGNANT, POWERFUL, AND AFFECTING."

—*Wilmington Sunday News Reader*

"Melvin Dixon's proven ability to create mosaics of movement and feeling, humanized by literary characters, is seen to its best advantage in *Vanishing Rooms*."

—*Metroland*

"A BRILLIANT EXPLORATION of . . . a world as complex and painful, as challenging and loaded, as that created by James Baldwin in *Another Country* and *Giovanni's Room*. . . . Melvin Dixon's novel of furious urban life stands comfortably alongside those by James Purdy, John Rechy, and Hubert Selby, Jr."

—Clarence Major, author of *Such Was the Season*

"The disturbing issues of racism and homophobia are forcefully examined in Dixon's provocative new novel . . . in which he skillfully illuminates the mixed emotions of distinctive urban characters whose lives are changed by tragedy . . . this realistic portrait of pain and loss carries strong emotional resonance."

—*Publishers Weekly*

"A POWERFUL PIECE OF WORK, with a message of humanity about people trapped in their skin, for better or for worse."

—*Milwaukee Journal*

BOOKS BY MELVIN DIXON

Vanishing Rooms (1991)

The Collected Poems of Léopold Sédar Senghor
    translation (1991)

Trouble the Water (1989)

*Ride Out the Wilderness: Geography and Identity
    in Afro-American Literature* (1987)

Change of Territory poems (1983)

Vanishing Rooms

MELVIN DIXON

A PLUME BOOK

I wish to thank the New York Foundation for the Arts for awarding me an Artist Fellowship in fiction which enabled me to complete this novel.

REGISTERED TRADEMARK—MARCA REGISTRADA

LIBRARY OF CONGRESS CATALOGING-IN-PUBLICATION DATA
Dixon, Melvin, 1950–
    Vanishing rooms / by Melvin Dixon.
        p.   cm.
    Originally published: New York : Dutton, c1991.
    ISBN 0-452-26761-7
    I. Title.
    PS3554.I89V36   1992
    813'.54—dc20   91-36317
                                                        CIP

Printed in the United States of America

PUBLISHER'S NOTE
This is a work of fiction. Names, characters, places, and incidents either are the product of the author's imagination or are used fictitiously, and any resemblance to actual persons, living or dead, events, or locales is entirely coincidental.

BOOKS ARE AVAILABLE AT QUANTITY DISCOUNTS WHEN USED TO PROMOTE PRODUCTS OR SERVICES. FOR INFORMATION PLEASE WRITE TO PREMIUM MARKETING DIVISION, PENGUIN BOOKS USA INC., 375 HUDSON STREET, NEW YORK, NEW YORK 10014.

for Richard

always

Where's taunted Christopher, sad queen of night?
And Ray, who cursing crossed the color line?
Where's gentle Brother Davis? Where's dopefiend Mel?
Let vanished rooms, let dead streets tell.

—ROBERT HAYDEN

PART ONE

Jesse

Metro wasn't his real name, but I called him that. It was fall of 1975. He led me by the arm out of the dark, rotting warehouse and to the pier fronting West Street. The sharp, fresh air cut through the smell of mildew stuffing my nose. The shock of the bright October sun made me blink so hard I missed a step and stumbled against him. He reached to block my fall, lifting my fingers to his nose. I squeezed his shoulders, held tight for a moment. We wobbled like two dancing drunks, vying for balance. His hands were shaking with a chill. The salt flavor of his skin left my mouth and my lips dried. I could stand and breathe again.

The lot around the pier and the warehouse looked like a deserted playground. Behind me I heard footsteps and creaking floorboards where we had been. We walked on ahead where the Hudson River lapped at soggy wooden piles. The water gurgled and sloshed with delight and the loose, stiff wood swayed in the dim flow. One post cracked free, bobbed in the sucking current, and floated away limp. I brushed off my jeans, more dusty now than blue. Wood splinters fell out of the seams. I looked at Metro to see if he noticed. His eyes were red and puffy. Maybe mine were too. His jeans were torn at the knees and just as dusty. Maybe his knees were scraped, I couldn't tell. He kept shivering, but I felt warm in the wide blade of sunlight. I squinted to see him clearer. My face wrinkled to a pout.

"Are you mad?" he asked me, brushing tangled brown

hair from his face. His hand pulled out splinters. "Are you mad because I made you come here?"

"You didn't make me come," I said. "I came because I wanted to."

Metro touched my denim jacket and let go. He shook his head. "Then why are you looking like that?" he asked, his eyes holding mine.

"Like what?"

"Like you're relieved or something."

"What's gotten into you?" I said. He stepped back from me. I didn't mean to sound so annoyed. His skin had never looked so white.

"Nothing."

"I don't want to meet here again, Metro. Promise me we don't have to meet here."

"Why should I promise? You call me Metro, don't you?"

"I'm scared, that's all." I wanted to touch him again, hold him close this time.

"You didn't say that a few hours ago."

"I know. I'm sorry I didn't."

I held out my hand, reached for him, changed my mind, and searched my pockets instead. I found my watch. It was three forty-five. Damn, I was late for dance class. Today was the day for improvisations, a good chance to make an impression before auditions next month. I couldn't miss a class. Metro started to say something, but I headed away from the warehouse to catch a crosstown cab. He followed after me, his keys jangling from a leather loop on his belt. "Wait," he said.

I couldn't wait. One cab zoomed by on radio call. Another stopped.

"Wait," said Metro.

"I'm late already, man, what is it?"

"Never mind. I just thought you were angry, that's all."

"I'm not angry." I got in the cab and lowered the window.

Metro had a wild look in his eyes. His chin held hard and straight. His thin lips opened and closed, but he said nothing more. He was taller than I but his shoulders slumped, and he looked weak. He didn't raise his shoulders.

"I'm glad I came, Metro."

"You didn't like it, did you?"

I smiled. And he smiled, hesitantly at first. I knew why I was there.

He stepped back from the cab. I said, "See you later, baby. I love you," and the cab lurched forward. The driver stared at me through the rearview mirror.

I'd be gone only a few hours. Metro would be home when I got back. Yet I missed him. My stomach fluttered. Maybe it was that empty, searching look in his eyes, or his suddenly pale skin against my oily brown hands. I missed him and searched the rear window. Metro was standing in the middle of West 12th Street, oblivious to the traffic veering around him. He scared me. I wanted the cab to turn around and pick him up, but it was too late. Why was I in such a rush? But I'm always rushing, rushing to dance class, rushing home, rushing to the mailbox, rushing just to be a quick step ahead of myself.

In no time I reached the studio. At my locker, I changed into yesterday's tights, which had aired out but should have been cleaned. Splinters fell out of my clothes, from the armpits of my shirt and the seat of my pants. I must have smelled of wood and low tide. Other dancers were warming up with stretches on the floor. I wasn't too late after all. Maybe I could sweat off the stink of the warehouse, dance with my feet on firm ground, not on creaking floorboards or with anonymous shadows lurking behind crumbling walls. Maybe the aftertaste of sweat, splinters, and Metro's tangled brown hair would go away. The other dancers wouldn't suspect a thing, I hoped, prayed. No one would know where I had been.

I stretched onto the floor for a few warm-ups, then stood with my stomach held in tight. My thighs eased open in demi-plié. Next, grand plié. I breathed deeply, calmly, and pulled myself up. On relevé I felt as tall as Metro, my hands as broad as his.

Anna Louise, the dance captain, called us into formation for single-file walks with our knees turned out, chests high. Next we lined up two by two. I found myself opposite another man, and we had to hold hands while doing triplet steps across the floor. For the next round I was with a girl I hadn't seen before in class, and another black dancer at that. She was shorter than I by a good foot, dark-complexioned with broad hips and close-cropped, boyish hair. But her legs were long, and she was some match for me in the quick, crisp steps we had to execute:

One-two-three   *One-two-three*
Up-two-three   *Down-two-three*

Before I had a chance to say hello we were across the floor again with a leap-two-three, leap-two-three. Waltz step, then turns. Between breaths I asked her name. "Ruella," she said heavily. "Ruella McPhee."

I reached for her hand and caught her wrist. "I'm Jesse Durand."

And we were back across the floor. Turns, leaps, waltz steps, and more stretches from head to toe.

Improvisation came next. "Just listen to this song for now, then let the music move you," said Anna Louise, her hands circling in the air. She held her hips and added, "At first I thought this song was so simple, but then the words and music started to make such terrible sense that I was taken with it completely. Now you try." She gave each pair of dancers a number.

We were number three.

The song played a second time. It was then that I recognized Nina Simone's voice crooning from the single phonograph speaker as if it needed more room, was aching for it. Her voice bounced upon the empty walls of the studio. The words were those of Waring Cuney, I later found out, from a poem that still plays in my mind:

She does not know
Her beauty
She thinks her brown body
Has no glory.

If she could dance
Naked
Under palm trees
And see her image in the river
She would know.

I looked at Ruella and smiled. My knees were already moving with what I wanted to say. Ruella was tapping her feet.
The song spoke to her too.

But there are no palm trees
On the street
And dish water gives back no images.

I thought of our house back in Hartford and my mother
Jessica, who named me. She made me and my older brother
Charlie wash dishes on alternate nights. We'd still fight over
whose turn it was. My father made us shovel snow, take out
the garbage in the cold, wash the car, scrub the kitchen floor,
rake leaves into a pile, but we'd jump in it and have to rake
them up again. I didn't mind the kitchen work, but I hated
the outside chores. "Work builds character," my father always
said. But he stopped preaching that line when he noticed my
preference for baking cakes and polishing silverware.

As the song ended plaintively, Simone's voice lifted high
in arabesque, her throaty tones like a bridge to cross.

When our turn came, Ruella and I held each other at
arm's length and circled slowly, measuring our steps and
each other. Our heads leaned in and out from the center
between us. Our bodies came close. We were drawn into the
music and the pain in Simone's voice. Our bodies were
swaying, singing. I broke the circle of our arms, held Ruella

in slight elevation, then eased her down. I spun away and
halted in demi-plié. She leaped in small quick steps, then
faced me. I lifted her straight up, felt myself lifting, too. I
brought her down slowly, carefully, my hands broad about
her waist. We stood side by side and bent legs, arms, and
thighs into a heap upon the floor. Her head eased into my
arms; our faces touched, hair caressed. We were almost one
head. We broke free and ran from each other like frightened
children. I curled into a ball and shot up in arabesque. Ruella
leaped high, then stood stock still. Our hands reached out,
held on, turned with open palms to the other dancers watching us. Our waists swayed, curled, stretched like whispers.
Our bodies had voices of their own, and they hushed into
quiet. We sank into a pile, rose up close together. Our tights
made our thighs one black pillar, and our Afros became one
huge head. We inched into separate positions, our hands and
eyes holding onto one another. The song ended with our
standing back to back like a Janus mask, facing both sides of
the room at once; one looking up and ahead, the other up
and behind. Quickly, on the beat, we changed sides for the
last wailing chord, then held firm as two sides of one body,
one voice, both of us dancing from whatever we made vis-
ible on the floor.

The class erupted into applause. Anna Louise came forward with her hands tapping out a beat in the air. "You'll
have to develop that into a polished piece," she said, "and
present it to us again. What do you say, class?"

The applause grew louder, filling us. I smiled at Ruella
who was grinning with such beautiful teeth. She smiled at
me distantly, then left the floor. When class finished for the
day, I waited at the dressing room until Ruella changed into
street clothes. We walked together to the subway.

"I felt something in that dance," I said.

"Me, too."

"Funny, isn't it?"

She looked at me without a word. Then she said, "I'm
not sure I know what you mean."

"Dance," I said.

"Yeah," said Ruella. "I've never been that close to a guy without feeling he wants something. You know what I mean?"

"Yes." Suddenly conscious of how I looked, I brushed off my jeans, pulled my stomach in.

"How do *you* know?"

"I just know."

Ruella looked at me hard, her eyes scratching at something. Sunlight glistened in her short hair. My scalp itched with splinters I couldn't wait to scratch out. "It was strange, but beautiful," she said. "Real beautiful."

I started giggling for no reason at all.

"Look," she said. "Forget what I said just then. I don't know you, really. You're charming."

"No, I'm not. Who wants to be charming, anyway?"

"Well, graceful, then. You move gracefully."

"Thanks," I said.

"Are you auditioning for the company, too?"

"I hope so," I said.

Below us a subway train screeched to a halt. Ruella looked worried. Her mouth grew tight. "Don't make me miss my train, now."

"I won't."

"I want to be home before it gets too dark."

"Let's get together again. To work on that dance," I said.

"I don't know, really. It was great, but I'm not sure I can get that high again. That's why I don't like improvs, not really. It's like, well, meeting someone, and after the rush of excitement, it's gone."

"What about the beginning of a friendship?" I asked, watching her.

She smiled, then tried to hide it.

"We can work on the dance, at least."

"Just the dance, Jesse?" Her eyes still searching. "I've got to get going."

"See you again? In class, I mean."

"Sure."

"How far are you going?"

"To the West Side. Eighty-fourth Street." Ruella bounded down the stairs. Then she was gone.

I wanted to dance again and to keep on dancing. The song and the improvisation came back to my mind, moving my feet as I walked home up 8th Street. My stomach was still contracted and made my steps light. I sang the song over to myself, trying to imitate Simone's raspy voice, but nothing but my own flat drawl came through. I thought of Ruella, then remembered Metro waiting for me at home. I changed more than the pronouns.

> He does not know his beauty
> He thinks his pale body
> Has no glory
> If he keeps dancing naked
> On the pier . . .

No, that's not it:

> There are no palm trees
> On the pier . . .

I must have laughed out loud because people started moving away from me on the sidewalk. Some went into the street. I kept singing and smiling. I'd tell Metro about the dance, about Ruella. In that brief moment she seemed to be a place to come to, a pier without splinters, a cozy room, not a warehouse.

I thought of Metro's thighs warm against mine, how close our faces held in making love, how wiry were his hands. But how lasting were those images? I walked faster. Suddenly, my toes were burning.

I reached the apartment, but he wasn't there. I waited for him through the early evening. I scrambled some eggs for dinner and read GQ twice. I waited for him through the night. I waited and waited. The more I waited the stronger was my desire for him. I wanted his hands on me. My legs still ached from dance, and when they relaxed I tried to sleep.

I wanted his hands on me. I didn't mind the cracked, chewed skin, the broken fingernails with flecks of dirt along the ridge. I wanted those hands on me, the blunt knuckles, the wrinkled skin, the bony joints, the tiny hair sprouts curling out. I wanted his hands on me. And wherever those hands led, I'd follow. I'd ride the tracks of his feet and the rough guardrails of those hands. Five fingers and five more. I wanted the electricity of his touch, his hands on me. How many times did I tell him, "Just touch me. Dance your fingers on my chest, my thighs. Press my flesh. Take off my clothes real slow." But when he touched me, my excitement dwindled into fear. His hands fluttered, suddenly unsure of themselves, of where they would land and do their marvelous work. I bent low and let his fingers drum on my belly. Then calmly they stroked where my secret skin was softest. He lifted away his hands and hid them. His lips found the tender places left aching by his touch. And when my hands kneaded him in turn—everywhere—nothing afterwards felt the same.

Then morning. An alarm shooting through me like the song. A knock on the door. Police.

They asked if Metro lived there with me and I said yes. They looked as if they expected me to be white or have something to hide. They told me to come with them downtown.

Metro lay in the city morgue. He had been stabbed eight times.

I couldn't look at him long. I couldn't breathe. I couldn't see. I grabbed for something to hold on to. The room whirled red, then black. The next thing I knew I was being lifted from the floor. When I could hold steady, they wanted to know his real name. My mouth was too dry to speak. Finally, in a voice hardly my own, I said, "Jon-Michael Barthé." His name didn't sound right at all. They probably thought I was lying.

Later they wanted my name. I said, "Jesse."

"Jesse what?"

"Jesse Durand."

"Ain't that a woman's name?" asked an officer behind a desk.

"Sometimes," I said.

They made me sign some papers. Then they let me go back home.

Once inside the apartment, I double-locked the door. I went to the window and spent hours looking up and down the street. Night came and swallowed up everything alive. Nothing moved, not even the subway below. I was alone. The rooms stirred empty. The emptiness gave off a chill. My eyes wouldn't cry and wouldn't close. I wanted to scream, but I had no air. I held myself in. I couldn't stop trembling.

God, what had happened? Just yesterday we were standing together at the pier, marveling at the polluted Hudson. Then I had to get to class, dance class. I thought I was late. There was the girl I had danced with. Then the hours and hours I waited for Metro to come home. Suddenly voices filled the outer hallway. Rushing footsteps. Laughter. Banging on doors somewhere. My hands shook again and my stomach tied itself in knots. Where could I hide? But the voices went past my door and up to the last floor of the building. I was sweating. I had to talk to someone. Anyone. I called my parents long-distance but there was no answer. I called again and the line was busy. But what could I tell them? College buddy, roommate, lover dead? Not a chance. Then I fumbled through the telephone directory, found her name, number, and I dialed.

"Ruella, this is Jesse. From dance class, remember? We met yesterday. We danced. Remember?"

"Yes, yes, Jesse. But how did you get my number?" I tried to say something but couldn't. "Jesse? You still there?"

"Listen, something terrible has happened. Metro, my friend. He's been stabbed. He's dead." I couldn't say anything more and she didn't say any more. My breath caught in the phone. "I can't stay here tonight," I said. "Not alone."

"You come right over, honey," she said. "I've got plenty of room."

I took only what I'd need for the night. Once there, I looked at her and she looked at me for a long time before I turned away and searched her windows. She didn't ask any questions. I wanted to talk, to tell her everything. She said there was no rush. I wanted to say that boys named after their mothers are different, that it wasn't for the money that they stabbed Metro; he had all his money on him when his body was found. It was for something else. When I tried to talk my lips started moving faster than the sounds, and I just cried, cried, cried.

Before the morgue's cold darkness had sucked me in, I had seen the gashes like tracks all over Metro's belly and chest. His open eyes were questions I couldn't answer. I couldn't say a word. The officer pulled the sheet all the way back and turned the body over where his ass had been slashed raw. I knew why he had been killed. I tried to scream but had no wind. I needed air. That's when I must have hit the floor. I could still see those gashes. They opened everywhere, grooves of flesh and blood, lips slobbering with kisses.

Ruella put her arms around me. My stomach heaved. I bolted for the toilet and vomited until there was nothing left of the bathroom or me. I woke up in her bed. From then on I called her Rooms.

After that first night she said I could stay longer if I needed to. I told her that guys like me are different.

"Then why did you call me?" she asked.

"Because you were there."

"But why *me*, Jesse?"

"We danced, that's all."

The second night Rooms touched me by accident. I didn't move. The chilly, October night filled the bed space between us. Then her hand crept to mine and held it, caressing and easing out the chill. Slowly, I relaxed but couldn't help remembering the men who had first made me warm. Metro's name came up raw on my tongue. It needed air, more air. "Metro," I said aloud. I kept still.

"Jesse? You all right?"

Rooms drew closer to me. We held each other tight against the dark.

"Jesse? You all right?" Her voice, hovering in the chill.

Something was pricking my scalp. I pulled out one splinter after another, but they were over all of me now, and I scratched and pulled everywhere. Not wood from the warehouse floor or the rickety pier, these were glinting steel blades with my name on them. Faces I'd seen before inched from corners of the room, closing the gap between here and there, now and then. Mouths opened and sneered. Teeth got sharp. Tongues wagged and breath steamed up around me until I sank into the sheets. Now a boy's voice. Then many voices. *"Jesseeeee."* A steel blade getting close. Closer. *"Jesse!"*

"I won't hurt you," said Rooms.

Outside the bedroom window, police sirens hollered up and down the streets. Where the hell were they *then?*

I imagined how Metro came up from the IRT exit and entered our block from the corner of West 12th and Bank Street. He passed the shut newsstand. It was almost morning. Metallic edges of light cut back the night. Metro walked with the same aching sound I knew from my own scuffling feet. I could almost hear the brush of denim between his thighs, see the arch of his pelvis as he swayed arms and hips as if he owned the whole street. His eyes tried to focus on the walk; his head leaned carelessly to the side. As he neared our building he was not alone. Other shapes crawled into the street, filled it. Cigarette smoke trailed out from an alley, and the figures of boys appeared out of nowhere, riding spray-paint fumes, crackling marijuana seeds, and waves of stinking beer.

Four, five, maybe six teenagers. Maybe they were the ones. The same ones I had seen before on my way home from rehearsals. Even then their smell of a quick, cheap high had been toxic. One time they spotted me and yelled, first one, then another until I was trapped.

"Hey, nigger."

"Yeah, you."

"Naw, man, he ain't no nigger. He a faggot."

"Then he a black nigger faggot."

They laughed. I walked faster, almost running, and reached my block in a cold sweat from pretending not to hear them. But I did hear them, and the sweat and trembling in my knees would not go away, not even when I reached the door and locked myself in.

Metro didn't believe it was that bad. But what did he know? A white boy from Louisiana, New England prep schools and college. "Don't worry, baby," he said when I told him what had happened. He held my head and hands until I calmed down. "It'll be all right." And we made love slowly, deliberately, believing we were doing something right. Still, I should have known better than to take so much for granted, even in Greenwich Village where we lived. And I should have known better than to leave him alone by the pier in the condition he was in, just for a dance improvisation. He had a cold, wild look in his eyes. How could I tell how many pills he'd taken? He could have fought back. But then why hadn't I fought back when those Italian kids started yelling, "He a black nigger faggot, yeah, he a faggot, a nigger, too," and shouting and laughing so close they made acid out of every bit of safety I thought we had? Now their hate had eaten up everything.

I could still hear them, making each prove himself a man—"I ain't no faggot. Not me, man"—and drawing blood. And when Metro left the black underground of trains and screeching wheels, when he reached for air in the thick ash of night, they spotted him like found money through the stinking grates of smoke and beer. I imagined how they followed his unsteady walk, his wavering vision, his fatigue. Curses like baseball bats swung out of their mouths. The first ones were on target: "There go a faggot."

"Hey man, you a faggot?"

Metro kept walking. Like I did. *Please keep walking. Please, Metro.*

"I say that man call you a faggot. You a faggot?"

Metro said nothing. Did he even hear them? They came closer. The streets were empty. No witnesses, no help. And I was back home waiting for his knock that never came.

"Yeah, you a faggot all right. Ain't he?"

"Yeah, he a faggot."

And Metro walked faster, skipped into a run, but they caught him. Knives slipped out of their pants. Hands reached for him, caught him in a tunnel of angry metal. They told him to put his wallet back. "This ain't no fucking robbery, man." They knocked him down. Metro sprawled about wet and hurt, couldn't pull himself up.

"Who stuck him?"

"Get up, faggot. We ain't through that easy."

"Look, he's bleeding."

"Who went ahead and stuck him before we all could stick it in? Who?"

They jostled him to his feet, feeling his ass.

"When can the rest of us stick it in? We all wanna fuck him, don't we fellahs?"

"Yeah. When can we fuck him?"

And Metro was wet from the discharged knives. He stopped treading the ground. He swayed back like wood in water, his eyes stiff on the open zippers. The leader of them grinning, his mouth a crater spilling beer, said, *"Now."*

"Why did you call me?" Rooms asked.

I said nothing.

"You think I'm gay, too?"

"No," I said.

"You really loved him," said Rooms.

"Yes."

"That makes all the difference." She held me with her eyes. They cut into me. "There's something else, isn't there? Something you haven't told me."

I tasted blood in my mouth. My head felt hot.

"I can wait," she said.

I went to her window and looked out. A subway rumbled underground, then it was quiet. The lump high in my throat, about to spread all through me since yesterday, eased down for a moment. I went back to my apartment to get the rest of my things.

Ruella

Now how many times have I told myself, "Ruella, girl, you really messed up." And how many times will I say it over and over again. I'd gotten the words right, the perfect lines to my one-woman show. The same lines, the same action, and yet, there I went falling for someone impossible and beautiful and already attached. You'd have thought I would have learned my lesson. Men. I was not to blame, really. Well, not for all that happened. Not for the despair in it or the desperation. I should have known better. I'd been miserable before. But that time, that one time I thought I could heal fast. My scars usually don't show, except for the tiny keloid behind my pierced ear. But that doesn't mean I don't remember losing anything. You can hurt on the inside without anybody knowing a thing. So what had I gotten myself into this time?

It was the grace of his feet on the hardwood floor, his toes touching mine. Right away I said to myself, "Ruella, girl, you better watch out." You know what I mean? It was just a demi-plié, an improvisation, not even the real thing, the danced dance. Which is why I hate improvs. Whatever suspicions I had during the triplet sequence with Jesse were confirmed in the improvisation. Without choreography, you have to rely on your instincts or memory. That's what gave me away. Jesse, too, I bet. Our instincts were magnets drawing us together. Left to ourselves, we dancers don't skitter about, we prance and prowl like cats. Dangerous cats. There's that sudden rush of movement, feeling, too, and it's gone too quickly. And when I felt Jesse lift me in an arabesque I did not expect but needed, I relaxed in his arms. I trusted him because no one had touched me about my waist as he did except my brother Phillip. I wasn't afraid. I knew he could take the weight. So Ruella, girl, why not twirl up your legs and let your heart follow one more time? It's the same count and you remember the moves only too well. And-a one-two-three-four-five-six-seven-eight!

What woman in her right mind would have expected Jesse or any man to call as soon as he did? Not me. I didn't give him my vital statistics on purpose. He wouldn't have heard me, anyway. By the time he got around to hinting he'd call, I had to run and catch my train. What girl wouldn't? It was long after rush hour, but the trains were crowded just the same, especially going uptown. And a good thing, too. I could stop thinking about him and that dance we did. Improvisation, sure. But we were saying something. Look out, Alvin Ailey! And just wait till those Taylor Johnson auditions. Hmmm. Truth is, I was tired, too. It was a long, hot ride, even in October. The three flights up to my apartment hadn't disappeared, and no elevator was installed overnight, so when I got in I just fell out. And you know what? I didn't even get to my yoga before that man was back in my mind again, with my legs going limp and fluttery all at once like I'm about to go on stage. I had noticed his eyes first, those lashes longer than mine, and roast-beef thighs that bent so easily into grand plié, his tights wrinkling at the knee. Sure he was watching me watch him. I wasn't a bit embarrassed. Then he started to sweat and the sweat greased that roast beef so slick, he looked delicious. I remembered my diet and looked the other way. I wasn't going to get involved.

Next thing I knew we were doing triplets across the floor: One-two-three. One-two-three. He tapped my shoulder. Said his name was Jesse-*two-three*. "Oh," I said, smiling, just to be cute and uninterested, as if I could lie right through these popeyes of mine with my teeth doing a kick-*two-three* out of my mouth, which is too big anyway. He took my hand and we were off across the floor–*two-three*. *One-two-three.* "It's not only a woman's name," he said as we joined a new line going back across the floor–*two-three*. By then, I was really grinning, letting all my teeth show. And since we were keeping good time, I decided to be bold. I said, "All the Jesses I've ever known have been men." He smiled again and danced closer–*two-three*. We headed back across the floor. "I'm Ruella McPhee," I said, trying to be as graceful as he, especially on the lift–*two-three* when you turn out your knees and lift your stomach high into the chest–*two-three*. That's when I started feeling something I shouldn't even have been thinking about. I brushed back my short hair, which didn't go anyplace, really, but the gesture made me feel rich.

Which is why I wanted to be a dancer in the first place. Gestures. Movement. Getting control of your body. Not like those times when I was a kid and couldn't stop crying for the itchy rash covering my ass and all I could do was a two-step in pain, hollering "Mama! Daddy! Phillip! Somebody help me!" The medicine wasn't working, and for the first time I was on my own, dancing solo around a waiting basin of hot water and salves that would tighten the skin on my butt and hurt even more. By the time I was grown nobody could see the rash, so I knew I could hide things. Like the keloid behind my ear no one could see. Not even my brother Phillip, who had left by then. It was Aunt Lois who screamed at me when I went ahead and had my ear pierced. She said it was vulgar. And when the keloid appeared, I knew it was her curse on me for acting so grown. But she never even saw it. I wasn't about to give her that satisfaction.

My two-room apartment is at the back of the building where it's quiet enough for me to meditate, do yoga, even dance with records playing loud with no trouble from the neighbors. Sometimes in the summer, I run in the park along Riverside Drive. It's not what you'd call jogging, my huffy-puffy high step, *up down two three*. That night, I was just too tired. I did my own warm-up stretches with the window open to let some of the October breeze off the Hudson keep me company. Then ballet positions: first, second, third. Old positions, new positions. Maybe tomato soup and green salad for dinner. Maybe some television. Get clothes ready for tomorrow, I reminded myself. I was doing part-time secretarial work three mornings a week until one o'clock. Then I was in one dance class or another for the rest of the day. I was hoping Jesse would be there next time. I wasn't just watching him. He was watching me.

And I wasn't going to think about him any more. I didn't need to get involved. Before you knew it I'd have to explain about the sitz baths and why my ass is three shades darker than the rest of me. But his hands had just the right tenderness I remembered from before when Mama and Daddy and Phillip took turns staying up with me and holding me when the rash on my butt burned too hot for me to lie down and sleep.

Then I did my yoga positions: right leg crossed into half-lotus, deep breathing. Cross left leg over. Breathe again. Cup your hands in the center of the groin, the center of concentration, energy. Inhale straight up into the chest. Exhale slowly, ever so slowly. Hands rest cupped at the center, elbows at ease on kneecaps. Let your thoughts come and go. Release them and breathe to a slow count—*two-three, one-two-three,* until you are empty. A memory came up and wouldn't leave until I gave it some space. The three count was me marking time to a tap dance. I was in front of two rows of skinny, awkward girls, all white, repeating after me, "shuffle-step, shuffle-step, heel-toe, heel-toe, heel-toe, heel-toe. Shuffle-step, shuffle-step, bend down, bend down, bend down, bend down." Our arms in a triangle, hands at the waist.

"And again," said Miss Goldberg.

We counted louder that time; she gave me another cue. "Now heel-step, heel-step, toe-step, toe-step."

"And again," said Miss Goldberg. "Again."

The repetition was killing us. Some girls couldn't keep up.

"Heel-step, heel-step, toe-step, toe-step."

My memories were ballerinas gliding in and out on point.

Just when I wanted to hold on to them, they were whisked
out of reach. But one memory hung around like the ugly
duckling left out of "Swan Lake," clucking and cackling in
my head. It was that freckle-faced Elizabeth whose mother
complained to Miss Goldberg about me, a black girl, leading
the dance steps and exercises. But she didn't say it like that.
Had to be sneaky with her evil. I was just too short, you
see, and the taller girls like her Elizabeth couldn't follow,
and my rhythm was throwing her off, making her mess up.
Never mind that the other girls could get it right. Miss
Goldberg ignored the complaint and kept me out front.
Somebody had to lead the dance of the six-year-olds or the
whole "Pixies in the Park" wouldn't go right.

Elizabeth's mother complained again. This time she
talked to other mothers who brought their knitting and *Ladies' Home Journals* to the waiting room until our hour of class
had finished. And just when we had learned the final kick-
two-three, lunge-two-three to end the piece in time for the
public recital at Cardinal High, the mothers threatened to
take their girls out of the revue. Miss Goldberg was fighting
mad, her face red as the ribbons on our tap shoes! She looked
like she was going to explode and set our high-waist tutus
on fire. "I'm the instructor here," she said. "I know what's
best." The mothers wouldn't budge. We girls stood
straighter in line than ever before. The mothers' anger hung
like a wall, measuring our lunge, kick, toe-step and bow.
Not one of us dared move.

Miss Goldberg tapped her foot real quick. She turned to
us, then back to the mothers. "All right," she said. "You'll
see for yourselves. We'll have two run-throughs. Elizabeth,
you lead first. Ruella, next." She sucked in her teeth and tut-
tutted her head back and forth. "All this just before dress
rehearsal, and the programs have yet to be folded. What
next?" She turned back to the mothers as we were lining up,
knees raised, hands on hips, feet ready to go. "Now watch,
all of you," Miss Goldberg glared. "Then tell me which one's
better."

I was scared. I took my old place at the far end of the

second row. Just then my mother walked in, took one look at me, and didn't say a word. She stared at me the whole time. Elizabeth started: "Shuffle-step, shuffle-step, toe-heel, toe-heel, bend down, shuffle-step." Her pace got faster and the directions she called out made us tap all off the beat. I had to stop cold when the girls in front backed up and those at the side headed right at *me* on the kick-two-three, turn-two-three. And if that wasn't bad enough, poor Elizabeth did the final lunge before the music had finished. Her mother stood up, mouth wide open, steely eyes ready to time-step Elizabeth's face all knotted up to cry. Everybody looked at them. Me, too. "Well," she said, turning from the mothers to us and back to the mothers again. "How was my Elizabeth to know? The goddamn record was slow. It wasn't her fault. Was it, Elizabeth? Stop that crying, Elizabeth, I'm taking you home. These people don't know anything about dance. Come on."

Then it was my turn. I was even more afraid. They all watched me, counted on me, and here I was trying to remember the right count. Well, the dance wasn't perfect, but we stayed in line. Our final lunge-two-three finished with the music. I didn't take a full breath until the mothers clapped and grinned their approval. My mother smiled that "silent victory" smile of hers and put her arms around my shoulders. The girls giggled and pinched me for luck, and we ran to change into our street clothes. I never heard my mother say a thing to the others. On the day of the recital, Elizabeth took sick. She never came back to our Tuesday-Thursday 3:30 class at Miss Beverly Goldberg's Contemporary Dance Emporium.

I blinked my head clear and moved on to a yoga headstand. Arms bent in a triangle on the floor, elbows pointed away, legs bent and moving up and up and over the neck. Headstand. Deep breathing. Relief, like salve on feverish skin. And I remembered how my skin cracked and bled. Mama had to coax me to sit in a basin of warm water. I screamed. Phillip rushed in and saw me crying through the hurt of the skin knitting itself back and my legs twitching.

Phillip saw me naked and didn't turn away in disgust at my blistered skin. He loved me like I was and made me feel pretty. Why couldn't other men be like him?

After ten minutes of yoga I was ready for soup and salad, television and bed. I had to be at the office before nine to open the mail and schedule appointments. I was already in bed when the phone rang and some man's voice came thick and raspy and nervous over the wire like he was calling long-distance. "Jesse," he said and waited for me to say something. Sure I remembered him. But how'd he get my number? He didn't say anything and I wasn't going to push because he sounded scared. Terrified. Something horrible had happened right in his neighborhood. His friend Metro, stabbed to death. Who wouldn't want to be with someone? I let him come right over. Why not? I had plenty of room. Two rooms. I didn't ask right away about all that had happened. When he came in he said he had no other safe place to go. I let him spend the night. I gave him my bed and didn't get in it until he was fast asleep. I saw how really handsome he is; so good-looking it's more than delicious, it's dangerous.

He slept like a dead man and never moved. In the morning I found him curled up like a sausage. He had Phillip's nose all right, and the same complexion. I dared myself to check it out. I went into my trunk, hidden under a flower-print cloth. I dug out Phillip's high school photograph and simply stared at it. And then his voice came back to me as calm as ever.

"Come on, Lil' Sis, the water's nice and warm."

"Naw."

"It won't hurt. You'll feel good and won't itch anymore."

"Naw."

Then Mama said I could have ice cream later.

"Naw," I said. The basin of water looked treacherous. But what did I know, a five-year-old in pain? I stomped and stomped, pumping my legs like pistons in an angry engine.

"Here, take my hand," said Phillip. "Take it."

I looked into his eyes, as round and clear as the basin of salves. His eyes were harmless so the water had to be, too. I took his hand. Phillip guided me like a partner in a waltz, back step, side step, one-two-three, one-two-three.

"Bend your knees," he said. "Nice. Nice. Good girl."

And with my eyes fixed on his and on Mama smiling behind him, I let Phillip ease me into the water and felt its cool caress on my fiery rash. My skin tightened, the itch subsided. The water was like silk covering me. I let out the air trapped in my chest.

Phillip was my first dance partner, until I learned to go solo, that is. Then Jesse held me in arabesque and eased me back to the ground.

Jesse was still asleep when I got ready for work. I wrote him a note that I'd be back at one o'clock. I set out some orange juice, instant coffee, and toast with a little butter on the side. Yes, he had Phillip's nose, and lips full of some flavor I hadn't yet tasted. But where is Phillip? He's put away safely now. Have you seen him? No. What have you done to him? Nothing. He's your brother, isn't he? I don't want to get involved. Girl, what are you hiding? I don't want to think about it anymore. Oh, Ruella, ain't you ever gonna learn? I guess not.

Y ou can't walk on 12th Street no more on account of the leaves covering the ground. Even in Abingdon Square just this side of Key Foods where only two or three maples give shade there are leaves everywhere, and when I walk outside I step on them. Some stick to my heels and scratch against the ground in a hurt voice. When it rains the leaves turn to mush and dirty my sneaks—not Adidas, but cheaper ones just as good. Even inside houses and buildings you got leaves brought in by all kinds of people. It's October, the season of yellow, copper, gray, and red, real red. The leaves are cut-off hands curling up like fists. If they grab for my sneaks, I just walk faster and harder to get them off. Like that faggot reaching for me out of the dirt and shedding red like some gray bone tree. You know the trees I'm talking about. You've seen them faggots. They all over this city like flies on shit. You hear the scratchy tumble of red leaves everywhere until someone rakes the place clean. Don't let nobody tell you that leaves don't talk. They pile up on you like something or someone is gonna burn.

The funny thing is whether it happened like you remember it happening or if your head changes it all, gets the people and action messed around. I'd talk to the other fellahs, but they'd think I was trying to punk out, see, and make like it was more than it was. Simple. We was getting back at him for trying to come on to me. You know, like I was some goddamn bitch. He probably wanted all of us, not just me, although we got him really scared by then, turning pale and twitching his eyes like he couldn't believe it was really happening to him out there alone at 4:30 in the morning in October. Wasn't he smiling at us? I remember his lips curling up, then down, his mouth moving like he was eating up the beer stink and smoke until he gagged. He acted weak, hungry, drugged up worse than the rest of us, but almost like getting fucked in the ass was an end to it. The hunger, I mean. I could tell he was hungry. We all could.

That night wasn't the first time I seen him. In fact, I seen him several times and knew where he lived. Sometimes I seen him go toward the docks and meat-packing houses. Why? Drink, maybe. There are a few bars around there where I've never been. He could have been one of the guys, you know, going after a six-pack at the corner grocery. He wore track sneaks—real Adidas—and jeans and a plaid flannel shirt opened from the neck on down. That day you could feel the season change right in the air, so I thought it was funny seeing the open V of his chest like that. The morning chill had cooled off what was left of Indian summer, but it was too early for leather jackets and thick collars. I thought he was one of the guys 'cause he didn't swish like them over at Sheridan Square that got makeup on or their hair too neatly trimmed around the neck. This guy walked like a regular fellah. Someone you'd want to talk to, or chase pussy or get shit-faced on Budweiser with, like we do most nights. Yeah, I seen him. Lots of times. Sometimes he didn't even know I was seeing him. Not until the day I was gonna meet Cuddles after his job when he actually came up close to me. It was near Cuddles' meat-packing house up by the docks and burned-out piers where Little West 12th Street runs into traffic on the downtown detour from the closed-up West Side Highway.

He's just walking and I'm walking. I look at him. He looks at me. I don't mean nothing by looking at him close like that, face to face. He doesn't look like no faggot. So I nod "Hey, man," and keep on walking. I mean, I want to be civil and shit. He might be able to lay me on to some drugs. But I say what I say, and he nods, and both of us go our separate ways. Easy, see. But damn, man, no sooner do I reach the door to Cuddles' job where he's supposed to be waiting but ain't, than I turn around and see that guy looking at me. He's watching my ass. Checking me out like you check out a bitch. Like he wants something from me. Needs it. Scheming how he's gonna get it. But he ain't making no moves. Cuddles finally comes outside and slaps me on the shoulder. I turn around and the guy is gone. Good thing, too. With Cuddles, I forget about him 'cause we're gonna get Maxie and Lou and ride around. I don't give a fuck about that guy looking at me.

Before joining the others, Cuddles and me have a beer where they don't check IDs. A little predrink drink. Get ready for the night. We always have good times. We tight, Cuddles and me. Cuddles' father makes him work after school. Trade school. My old man died too soon to make me do nothing. Half the time I live in the streets. I should quit school, get a full-time job. Get the cash Cuddles has most times—where I got to ask my Moms to spot me some coins, mostly for cigarettes. Don't need no subway fare. Just jump the turnstile soon as the train screeches in. I do the best I can. Cuddles is the one in the money. Ain't tight-assed about it either, which is why we hang together. I like him better than Maxie or Lou, but I can't tell them that, not even Cuddles, 'cause he'll start calling me names and picking on me 'cause I'm only fifteen and he's older. Just a little older.

"Two drafts, what d'ya say?" I tell him.

"Just what I need. Throat's tight as a damn drum."

"Mine's like a hose, man. Only it's empty."

"What's eating you? I been working all day."

"Shit, man, this dude, you know, like the rest of them in the Village. Always coming on to you, checking you out like you some bitch."

"They think it's their turf, Lonny. We just tourists, you know."

"Yeah. Faggots is everywhere."

"You ain't got nothing to worry about, long as they keep a distance."

"But this dude acted like he wanted it and could get it."

"He say anything to you, man?"

"Naw, he just kept looking."

"He touch you, Lonny? He touch you?"

"Why you wanna know?" I say, but nothing else, just set my jaw tight so he'll know not to fuck with me. You can never tell about Cuddles. Always fucking with somebody.

"Drink up, Lonny. The guys gonna be mad 'cause we got a head start." Cuddles slaps me on the shoulder and ruffles my stringy hair.

I'm grinning now, feeling stupid, too.

"I know what you need, man," he says. "Let's get the rest of the guys and blow outta here."

I don't say nothing more to Cuddles and just "Hey, man" to Maxie and Lou waiting for us at the motorcycle garage in Chelsea. Lou has his machine up on the racks and comes toward us, wiping the grease off his hands. Maxie sits on a locked bike and leans forward and back like he's speeding down I-95 and going into a long S-curve. He thinks he's in some kind of pro race, but ain't none of us old enough for the big time yet. Some places you got to be eighteen. I'm just a year away from quitting school if I want. Maxie is out of school already, but he don't have a job. Maybe 'cause his round pink face is full of acne. Cuddles is blond and older than me by a couple of months. He's funny, and you never know if he's gonna turn on you, especially if he can act big around Lou and Maxie. Lou is eighteen and works at the cycle garage where we hang out. I usually get Cuddles after his job 'cause he's near where I live. We walk the rest of the way. Sometimes Cuddles has his moped and we ride over. Junior cycle, we call it. Wish I had one.

Once I stole a ten-speed and spray-painted it over. I rode around, got Cuddles, and we rode double, Cuddles peddling and me on the seat, my hair blowing into spikes behind me and me holding Cuddles at the waist with my feet spread out from the double chain and derailer. He told me not to hold on so tight. Lou laughed his nuts off at us riding up to the garage on a stupid bike like that. He called us silly shitheads. I didn't care since he's mostly friendly with Maxie and thinks we just punks anyway. That's when Cuddles tried to act tough. But when I told Lou how I stopped this kid in the park on the East Side, took the silver ten-speed right from under his ass, raced downtown, and spray-painted it red, he looked at me weird like he didn't think I had the balls to do shit like that on the East Side. "You a mean dude," he said. And I said, "Naw, just regular white trash." I grinned all over myself and slapped his palm. Slapped Cuddles on the palm too.

This time, walking up on the guys already at the garage and with me feeling the slow buzz of brew on a warm day, I don't say much to Lou or to Maxie 'cause Cuddles is already talking big and laughing. Then I get the drift of some shit that really puts me out. "Man, what Lonny needs is some pussy," Cuddles is saying. "He ain't had none in so long he's watching the boys on Christopher Street." And Cuddles laughs, poking me in the side like I'm supposed to laugh too. But I'm hot in the face, red all over, itching to dance on somebody. But shit, Cuddles my man, or supposed to be. He can turn on you and get Maxie and Lou on his side. Like the time we was fussing and Cuddles jumps in, mocking me, saying, "One minute you talk like us, the next minute you don't. You trying to fuck with us or something?" Then he jabbed his finger in my chest. "Either you one of us or you ain't." Now they're all laughing like they got something else on me.

"No shit. You mean Lonny's sneaking after some faggot pussy?" says Lou.

"Maybe Lonny just getting tired of the front door," says Maxie. "He wants to come 'round the back."

"Can't get it open no more, huh, Lonny?" says Lou.

They make me feel like shit. I probably look like shit too. Damn Cuddles, I could kill him. Punch them all out. Why he have to goof on me like that when I'm enjoying my buzz? When these guys start loud-mouthing, no telling what they gonna do. "Naw, man," I tell them, "The only thing I do with a back door is shut it with my fist."

"You into fist-fucking!" Maxie screams. I don't even know what he's talking about. Then he balls up his greasy hands and starts waving them all in my face like I'm gonna stand there and take it.

My hands get tight, maybe tighter than his. What I got to lose? "Yeah—and if you don't watch out, I'm a fist-fuck yo' face!"

"Whoaaa," Maxie hollers, pretending to fall down, his mouth and eyes shooting open.

"Whoaa," says Cuddles, slippery as spit.

Then Lou goes, "Aw man, we just messing with you. We know you cool."

"Yeah, he cool," says Maxie. "When you got a shitty dick, you gotta keep cool, and clean."

That's when I pull him off that locked bike where he thinks he's king or something. Get him down tight between my legs, face red, and I'm about to beat his pink acne head to a pulp when Cuddles and Lou pull me back by the hair. I'd lose anyway. Maybe Cuddles and Lou know something I don't know.

"Cut the shit, man."

"Yeah, cut it."

I let him up. Maxie brushes himself off real calm like it was nothing but a punk like me getting out of hand. Being naughty. Shit. I push him away. "Next time you wanna give some lip," I'm saying—and I grab my cock in a mound, point it at him—"wrap your lips around *this.*"

"Whew," says Lou. "You don't need no taste that bad."

"Let's get the fuck out of this garage," says Cuddles. "Who's buying this time?"

We head for Key Foods and load up on two sixes. We get our regular bench in Abingdon Square which tries hard to be a park with a little grass and dirt, but it's mostly concrete benches and jungle gyms. We sit and sip and sit and sip. Can't wait for night to come, and I'm still trying to be cool. It ain't always bad, drinking with the guys. About what I dig most these days, biding time till I can quit school. Be out on my own. More time to hang out. We get so plastered sometimes that night comes up on us with a scare and you wonder where the day went. Night is all right by me in the summer, but in October, man, you see things start dying all over the place. Not just red leaves circling down from the trees, but the cold whooshing in, cleaning the air of summer dog shit and roach spray. I can tell it's gonna be an early winter. Long one too. Sooner than anyone expected, October came in, screaming, like an old lady afraid of burglary or rape. Like the skinny black dude who had the shit scared out of him when the guys stopped him and called him a nigger faggot to his face. Wish I coulda seen that.

On the concrete bench next to me Lou says beer and night get him horny. His eyes snap at any piece of ass walking by. "Not any piece," he says all loud and blustery. "Just the ass that squats to pee." He starts stroking himself and gets up, saying he got to have some woman, and beer sprays from his mouth. Maxie says he needs some woman too. They say "woman" cause they won't get anything calling it pussy. Cuddles stands next to Lou, holding him up then pushing him aside. "Forget about the woman," Cuddles says. "I just want some snatch." He poses like a hero out of some spy flick or war movie. I listen to them laughing and cackling, but I don't say nothing about women or anything else.

"Listen, if we all put our money together—"

"What money," I say. "I just blew what I had on the beer."

"See, I told you he was small," says Maxie.

"Shit."

Cuddles says he got ten dollars left. "And I got ten," says Lou. "Twenty's enough."

"Ain't a bitch in town for that amount," I say. Nobody answers. Every time we start cutting up on beer or herb or cycling around, somebody gets horny and we end up talking about bitches and chasing leg.

"Drink up," Cuddles tells me.

"Let's blow back to the garage," says Lou. "Then the road to heaven."

We split up, riding double.

"Hey, Lonny," Maxie goes. "Don't hold so tight."

"Sorry."

I feel bad not having any money, but that's all right with the guys. We don't go to a house or a place with rooms. We ride uptown, along Broadway, near 79th Street where Cadillac headlights dim and slow to a cruising speed. Ten blocks further you see the bitches in miniskirts, all legs and face and not much chest, which is fine with me. Maxie pulls to a curb where Lou and Cuddles are leering at somebody. I stay at the bike while Maxie walks over to them. Suddenly she's laughing out loud like they was the funniest thing she's ever seen. She waves her hands away and goes back to her pose in the door of a bakery that's closed for the night. Maxie goes ahead a half-block further and approaches another and another one until he comes running back to us.

"Any go?" Lou asks for all of us. Me included.

"Yeah, some bitch around the corner at ninety-first. You guys down?"

"Yeah," Cuddles says and looks at me. I say yeah, too.

We go on up to 91st Street and turn east between Broadway and Amsterdam. We stop at the first abandoned building which is really near Columbus. The woman—I'll say "woman" too this time—has dyed blond hair that looks like straw under the street lamp. She pulls at her skirt and pops gum in her mouth. "Hurry up now," she says. "I ain't got all night. For this little shit money, I'm doing you a favor. Be glad I got the real money early. Roscoe be on my ass if he finds out. Be on all your asses, too."

She enters the dim hallway and Maxie and Lou follow her up to the first floor. I wait with Cuddles against the parked cycles. They're gone only about five minutes when she comes out again. "Anybody got a jacket? It's damn cold in there."

Cuddles hands over his jacket. Up close now I see she's not much older than me, maybe younger. I wonder why she's doing this. I want to say something to her but I don't. Besides, what can I say? I'm here. Cuddles winks at me and

points to her swaying ass as she goes back inside. We wait.
When our turn comes Maxie and Lou watch the bikes. Cuddles goes first. He doesn't take off his pants all the way, just
unzips his fly and plows in. He's fast. Faster than I'll ever
be. Maybe. It's already my turn. Her face turns up to me
from the floor, her eyes tiny like they're holding something
in. "What's the matter? You scared?"

I don't say anything. I make my eyes tiny, like hers.

"If you don't come on, you lose. Ain't no discounts,
now." And she laughs. Cuddles laughs, too. I climb on top,
my clothes tight at the waist. I feel around her titties and she
turns her tiny eyes away from me, arching her back. "Stop
fumbling with my chest. Ain't nothing there." I want to say
I like it like that, but I don't say nothing. This close I can
see her teeth ain't clean.

Cuddles moves toward the door, keeping a look out. I
try to say something, but she starts moving her hips around
and my dick pops out of my pants. The tightness is gone.
I'm all in her now and working, watching her face, her head
shaded by the denim jacket and her tiny eyes doing nothing
until they open up on me doing what I'm doing.

Cuddles comes over and just stands there like I'm taking
too much time. Shit, he got his. I'm getting mine. He watches
me. I try to say something, anything. His eyes hold me. Her
eyes pinch tiny again, and I feel the pull way down between
my legs. I get it in my throat and say, "You see me, Cuddles?" And he says, "Yeah man." The girl breathes deeply,
but she don't say nothing. It's just me and Cuddles. Me and
him with words. "You see me getting this pussy?"

"Yeah, I see you, man."

"I'm getting it. I'm getting it, Cuddles." And my head
goes light all of a sudden as if a weight was easing off me
and going her way, maybe his. My hands grip the ends of
the jacket like they're the spokes of a wheel turning me. My
head circles faster than my body or her head below mine as
I push my face against the cloth and away from her tiny eyes
and straw hair. I feel Cuddles' eyes on me again, then her
eyes on me. The smell of denim and armpits make me tingle

all over and tingle again until my whole body heaves and pulls. The jacket lets go the smell of grease and body all in my face, and I can't do nothing but let go myself. The bitch had nothing to do with it. Riding on empty, I ease up. She smooths her skirt back into place. I don't say nothing and she don't say nothing. We walk outside.

Maxie hands her the twenty dollars. She looks like she could cast a spell. "You better be glad Roscoe ain't around. He'd be on all your asses for this lousy twenty bucks."

We rev up for the ride downtown. Cuddles brushes off his jacket and climbs behind Lou at the handlebars. "I was just shitting you, Lonny, about that faggot stuff. You cool, man. I seen you. You cool."

"I know," I tell him. "I know I'm cool." I slap him on the back. I climb up on Maxie's bike. I ain't grabbing tight this time. In a minute we're gone.

Jesse

What was I doing eighty blocks uptown with this woman whose eyes were windows on me? How did I get here? Took the A train to 59th Street, changed to the Broadway #1 local, got out at 86th Street, and walked two blocks south, two blocks west. Watched for traffic leaving the West Side Highway and came this close to jumping into the filthy Hudson.

Inside, Rooms asked me, "You were lovers for a long time?" She joined me on the couch. It was her couch, her apartment.

"Yes."

"I can't imagine what it was like."

"Neither can I, sometimes," I said. "No, that's not true."

"I didn't think so," she said.

I left the couch and paced the floor, then touched the windows. The walls were full of posters of dancers and company tours. Metro and I never got around to decorating our walls. They stayed bare and white.

"You want to talk about it?" said Rooms, following me with her eyes. I went back to the couch and took her hands, feeling the grains of her knuckles as I spoke.

I had signed the lease on the apartment on West 4th Street a few weeks before Metro and I finished college. It was a three-room walk-up close to the IND lines at 14th Street and 7th Avenue where the 1, 2, and 3 trains run. I had studied the subway map, memorized the numbers and color codes of the train routes. Metro had to visit his family and arrived in Manhattan two weeks after I moved in. He figured out the routes for the BMT, the IRT, and the IND, the bus lines and the shuttle system faster than I did. He had been to Paris where they have a better network, they say.

This was our first year living together. The rooms were small but had four windows and two exposures. I could watch the sun rise and set. Our bedroom was large enough for only the bed and a tiny desk where Metro wrote when he worked at home. "You couldn't find anything larger?" he once asked.

"Nothing we could afford," I said. My nerves danced as he fretted from one small room to the other, the kitchen-dining-living room, the bedroom-study, hall, bathroom, closet, and back again. Metro was always moving. He wouldn't sit still, even to talk about moving from these rooms to somewhere else. Maybe he should have been the dancer and I the news reporter. But he had a journalist's eyes and wanted to take in everything, be everywhere. Just like that day at college when our eyes first met at Clarkson Hall. Now that he's gone, I can't help wondering what he really saw, or what I saw. All I remember is that our eyes were hungry.

That cold February morning made the sun stand still. I was up at dawn. It was February 21, the day we declared Malcolm X Day. Since the college wouldn't cancel classes to memorialize Malcolm's death, we black students would. From the top story of Clarkson Hall, the main building at Wesman University, hung a large bed sheet with the words, "Malcolm, Malcolm" streaked in black spray paint, flapping against the frost. It was a sign of our presence at the university and a measure, so we thought, of our strength.

Desks, chairs, and portable blackboards were stacked as barricades at the front and back entrances. We were more afraid of the jock fraternity next door than the police. By eight o'clock, when the first classes were to be held, over a hundred of us had filed into the building, filling the halls and foyer and front windows on every floor. I took up a post on the second floor. From the outside the building must have looked totally occupied. At least, that was the impression we wanted to give. I saw white students and a few blacks gathered outside; some paused and just walked away, bewildered. Some I knew from dance class, the dormitory, the theater. Many were simply confused, astounded perhaps that the building had been taken and that black students were now in charge. We were honoring a fallen hero, a symbol of something we had but didn't quite have, and needed to have. Some radical white students gathered with picket signs, expressing their support. By noon more students had congregated outside than there were inside. Someone quickly arranged an impromptu rally. A few student writers read from their poetry. One of the organizers asked me to dance something "political," but I declined, remembering his look of disdain when I first said I was studying to be a dancer, not a doctor or lawyer like the rest of them. From my window post in the empty classroom I looked out and did nothing more than watch.

What I saw scared me. It was my history professor, Robert James Woods, hurrying angrily along the front of Clarkson. He was determined to hold his class elsewhere. He stopped at the barricade, looked up at all the windows. I saw him, but he looked at me without any hint of recognition. And I always sat in the front row of his class. We must all have looked like mold on brick to him. He turned away disgusted. I remained at the window, stunned. Then I saw someone else. Thick, wavy brown hair, angular forehead and chin, horn-rimmed glasses, stubby fingers clutching a reporter's steno pad. Eyes like reaching hands. When he looked straight at me, I felt pulled into his whole face. His stare made me feel weightless, light, angled toward him on wings suddenly fluttering from inside me and begging for air. I wanted then to get under his skin, travel at breakneck speed through his veins and right to his heart. But there I was, locked inside the building, barricaded away on the second floor. So I waved to him slowly, with all the fingers of one hand. He nodded and waved back. His hands were much larger than I thought.

I couldn't wait for the demonstration to end. Malcolm X was of little help, and students kept playing records of his speeches that echoed through the halls. I moved from window to window, from one empty classroom to another. The reporter was moving too. I watched as he spoke to the picketing students and the worried administrators while jotting notes on his pad. And I watched him follow me as I moved. When we found ourselves staring again, I knew we would meet somehow on the outside. The takeover suddenly became the dullest event of the day. My hands felt empty with nothing to touch.

When at last it was time to leave Clarkson, after hours of negotiations between the administration and leaders of the Black Student Union, after flashing bulbs and whirring television news cameras, we were told to keep quiet about our actions, especially the planning, but what did I know or remember by then? The barricades were lifted. Light and air rushed into the crowded hallway. We formed a line in threes, males on the outside, women in the middle for protection. Then silently, just as night was coming on, we left the building.

Reporters gathered close about us, but we kept marching away from Clarkson and toward the Nkrumah African-American Center. Our silence was really a prayer for safety. None of us wanted to be expelled or disciplined. Besides, most of us were on scholarships. My parents would have killed me if they had found out what I had done. Cameras clicked. Our feet crunched the hard, leftover snow. I tried not to look for the wavy brown hair or the horn-rimmed glasses, but there he was, following along my row. I knew he would ask me something. My eyes begged him to. I wanted to talk, but not about Malcolm X or the demonstration. I wanted to talk about him and me, about what I saw from the second-story window and he from the snow-capped street.

He caught up to me, his words as breathless as my stride. "I'm from the *Wesman Herald*. Can I talk to you for a minute?"

I said nothing, but I could feel talk rumbling up from my belly.

"Just one question, please. How did you all get inside?"

No answer from me; my stomach now a tunnel at rush hour.

"How many of you were really in there?"

No comment. Blaring traffic jam inside me.

My feet weighed heavier and the Nkrumah Center seemed miles away. He tried to keep pace. Others marching behind me were gaining upon us and crowding him out. He dropped his note pad. I looked away from him and kept marching, my stomach moving faster than my feet.

"Dammit," he said. Then his voice slipped back and was suddenly different. "How y'all expect people to listen to you if you don't communicate?"

Communicate? Y'all?

From the byline of his article in the campus paper the next day, I learned his name was Jon-Michael Barthé. With an accent. Later, I saw him in the cafeteria line and told him my name. We talked. He was from the South, he said. And he had been to Paris the semester before. I hadn't been any-where, really. I invited him to my room for more talk. We said nothing about the takeover or about Malcolm X. We talked about ourselves and the stupid grin all over his face and mine. And for the first time he brought my trembling hands to his face. The smoothness of his skin unsettled me. Worried me.

"That's romantic," said Rooms.

"What do you mean?"

"Seeing Metro from the classroom window. Becoming friends. Touching like that."

"It wasn't easy," I said. "The black students thought I had betrayed them. It was bad enough being a dancer, but a white boy's friend? No way."

"Then there's something more," she said. "Something you're not telling me."

I didn't know what else to say.

Metro and I finished college on a rainy spring day. Then we danced together on the sharp, metallic edges of Manhattan. Windows, steel, even the rooftops glittered in the sun, and our eyes were hungry for all we could see. Graduation day had released us from the confinement of Connecticut, the carpeted green of the campus quad, the terror of discovering what and who we were, the lonely aftermath. But we had finished college; the four years were gone. As we marched to receive our diplomas, cameras clicked from all sides, and it was then that I met Metro's parents for the first time. "Smile, son," his mother said as her camera reached for him. Metro stepped back and away from me, his smile tired and lazy from last night's celebrations. His lips were chapped, his eyes wild and open with no bright luster calling me into them like before. He took a long step back from me, then came close. I said, "Well, we made it, man," and he said, "Yeah," and I hugged him. We waved our diplomas at the cameras snapping from his folks and mine. I rolled my parchment and hit him with it, and he hit me. We tussled and danced in our gowns, hollering ourselves silly. I bowed to him. He pulled wide the edges of his sleeves and curtsied. There was a lot our families didn't know about us.

His parents made him return to Louisiana with them for a couple of weeks. I went ahead and moved to Manhattan. I waited for him. When he joined me, he looked scared and different. I'll never know what happened down there. But he did say how he remembered something in his growing up. Once Metro had gone along when his mother drove their maid Bertha home, which was far out in the country. I don't know how old he was then, but he remembered smelling woodsmoke and tobacco everywhere. When their car pulled into Bertha's yard, one of her sons ran up to look in at Metro and his mother. His name was Otis, Bertha said, and the boys shook hands. On the ride back home, Metro told me, he kept smelling woodsmoke and tobacco. And when his mother wasn't looking, he sniffed, then tasted, where Otis's hand had touched his.

He joined me in Manhattan and began work. He had the

night shift at the *Daily News* and started out editing press releases and drafting celebrity obituaries in advance. I took as many dance classes as I could. I worked off and on with a new choreographer who was experimenting with geometrical shapes, triangles and squares formed from human bodies in motion. But most of the time I was darting from one technique class to another, often without a moment to change out of the tights under my jeans. Metro slept during the day or freelanced articles for art magazines. We'd make love in the late afternoon before he went to work. By then I'd be supple from the day's exercises. He'd open my fist and smell the palm of my hand. Sometimes we made love in the early morning when the city night was just beginning to dissolve. I'd say things to him like, "Metro bringing me into the sunlight. Metro, my underground man." And he'd say, "Take it, baby. Take it all."

The night work was slowly wearing him down. He was getting pale, growing silent and distracted when we were together. His parents kept after him to come back South. He started taking pills, uppers to keep him going, downers to help him relax. He was staying out later than his work required. I knew he went cruising sometimes and was sleeping around. So was I, now and then. But he started wanting more than I could give. One day, one night, rather, he called me from a phone booth on West Street. When I joined him there, I found him haggard, thin, and with puffy, sleepless eyes. He led me to a warehouse along the pier that had long ago been abandoned.

"Don't say anything, Jesse. Just follow me." His voice had changed.

He led me to a door and inside where it was dark and reeking of beer and marijuana. Floorboards poked up here and there, and the smell of the river was strong. There was another room above this one, and we climbed a flight of rickety stairs.

"You like it?"

"What kind of place is this anyway, Metro? What are we doing here?"

"A friend from work told me about it."

"But this place stinks," I said. "It's dangerous. You can't even see anyone." And I couldn't see anyone, but I heard footsteps and whispers, saw glowing cigarette butts, the fast flame of a match. Far from us and over part of the river was a hole in the ceiling, then the roof. The whole place looked like it could collapse in a minute.

"People come here," Metro said, "to play."

"I don't want anything to do with this. Let's get out of here." I moved to leave but couldn't find the stairs, and when I did, I didn't trust them to hold me.

"Jesse, please. Look, things go on here. All the time." Metro pulled me further inside. Shadows moved about. A beer can dropped and spilled. Floorboards creaked. A chill crawled into my back.

"Look Metro, we have our own place. You and me, right?"

He said nothing.

"What's gotten into you?" I asked.

Metro looked away from me, disappointed. Then his eyes brightened. He started to laugh. "Don't you see? All this is part of it, what we came to New York for. The streets, the sweat, beer and cigarettes. And here? You'd walk in, any-body would walk in, hands hooked in the belt, your jeans torn just so around the crotch. You'd lean against the wood, and I'd find you, smell you waiting there. I'd kneel just so, and you'd talk dirty to me." He laughed again and his voice chilled me. I couldn't tell if he was serious or not, and that scared me all the more.

"I don't like this," I said. "Not at all." I left him standing there and waited for him downstairs and outside. To my right was another pier, but without a warehouse, just row after row of blackened beams. And there were people, a few men in jeans, some drag queens. Some had on the slightest of clothes, some were bare-chested, booted, jeans torn through. But I was the one who felt empty, filling up with loss. I couldn't help thinking how in just a short time the city had separated Metro and me. First by the hours of our work, our lovemaking when everyone else was taking the morning subway. Then by the things we saw each day: I had lofts and mirrors and leotards and dance barres bending me one-two-three, one-two-three, and opening my thighs in deep pliés. Metro had the police files, the city morgue, night court, three-alarm fires, subway muggings, and obituaries. The lines of his face were becoming tracks of frayed nerves and sleepless nights, even after making love, and we were withdrawing to separate sides of the bed, the tiny bedroom, the three-room apartment, and finally the street.

He asked me to meet him there once again after work. It was early, early morning. The place was still dark as if morning had changed its mind or had merely taken flight at what it saw. I was scared. When I found Metro and held him close, away from the loose beams and crumbling floorboards, I didn't suspect it would be the last time I'd see him alive. I can still feel the splinters in my skin.

"That's still not all," said Rooms, watching me more closely than before.

"What do you mean?" I tried to look away. Her eyes found mine. We watched each other cautiously, then with care.

"You made it to class all right," she said. "And we danced. Remember?"

"Yes, we danced."

The police said they were investigating the attack. They had a few leads. "It wasn't just an attack," I argued. "It was murder." They had notified Metro's family who had his body shipped to Louisiana. I didn't go to the funeral. I stayed inside where I was. The night they buried him, I took the #1 train downtown and walked to the pier. I was too afraid and ashamed to go further. And he was all I could think about.

Metro wasn't even his real name. I just called him that.

Now the emptiness in my chest whistled with his name and mine. But what about Rooms?

Rooms, where I tried to lose myself.

I told her I know how it feels to have a man inside you. I know how to fuck and to be fucked, how the pain and the release can make you dance in place. Hop-step and dip. My name is Jesse. My mother's name. See how easily I open? See how deep the cuts run? I've had a man from the inside, under the skin, deep, deep inside me.

"Why are you telling me this, Jesse?"

"Because I have to, I don't know."

She said she liked it when I called her Rooms. We exercised and danced together until our sweat ran in streams on the floor of her apartment. With Rooms I found other spaces to touch, other windows to look from. But there was one locked door. Metro had the key, and he was dead.

"Why did you come to me in the first place, Jesse, if you felt so sure about Metro? About yourself?"

"I had to know."

"Know what?"

"If they took everything from me when they killed him."

"You're very strong there, and beautiful."

"I mean inside, Rooms. My feelings inside."

"You'll find different feelings, maybe."

"You think so?"

"Here," she said, stretching her thighs. "Here."

Ruella

Well, I thought, why not come right out and let him know you're interested? There's nothing wrong with that. It's like planting a seed or warming up before a dance. But that's not all I said. I told him my real name, Ruella McPhee, and he still called me Rooms. Don't ask me why. I was a place to come to, fine, I accepted that. But English isn't the only language I know. How else could I pretend to be a foreigner and get such attentive customer service in those Fifth Avenue shops on payday? Cardinal High was good for something practical besides typing class. So I told Jesse, "*Rue* is the French word for 'street.' That means I'm going somewhere." Then he said something smart like, "Metro runs underground, gets under the skin, too."

"I wouldn't know about that," I said, with my eyes arched.

That made him blush.

"And *ella* is Spanish for 'she.' So I'm a woman going somewhere. Bet you can't even say it, huh? Eh-yah."

"Fast travel," he said. "Caroom-boom-clack, caroom-boom-clack."

"Not on my train, pretty poppa," I hollered. "I need me an easy rider."

That shut him up, but after a minute he grinned like he'd caught me in my own mess. "Then we'll make it nice and easy."

"Clickety-clack?" I asked.

"Eh-yah."

Chile, my legs like to fall out from under me. But I didn't tell him that.

Truth is, I'm not a pretty woman. Not really. People say I'm pretty when I smile, so I keep smiling, even grin to give my teeth some air. So I didn't expect Jesse to call. I never had long, even hair. The kind you pet or sing verses to while combing it out. I'm not that tall either. Medium. Well, short to medium. It took me five years of tap dance and modern to get my leg muscles strong enough for ballet. Then I thought I'd die before getting my first pair of toe shoes, those pink satin ones with the roll of rabbit fur to wrap around the toes and those long shiny ribbons reaching half-way up the calf. Then I was on my way. Going somewhere, if only to another dance class. Jesse and I, being very colored and almost late, wound up as partners.

That's how we met. We danced. Triplets *one-two-three* across the floor, and a long, improvised movement to Nina Simone's heavy voice. I hadn't seen Jesse before, so how was I to know we were more alike than either of us wanted to admit. Besides, where would it lead? I've known men like him before, who were interested only in their bed or mine. So we just danced, Jesse and I. Nothing more. I had the feeling we'd see each other again, maybe become friends. And when he needed a place to stay, how was I to know he'd remind me of my older brother Phillip, who used to hold my hand while Mama raked the comb through my knotty hair and made me holler. And when I had to see the skin doctor for the burning rash on my behind, he'd hold me close and say with the tenderness of God, "Hold on, Lil' Sis. Everything's gonna be all right." The only person I could believe in through all those salves and creams and itch was my brother Phillip. And here comes Jesse pulling me across the studio floor on a leap-two-three, turn-two-three, relevé, and down.

Jesse must have thought about himself in that improvisation. Perhaps about Metro, too, who was alive then. Alive in Jesse like Jesse made Phillip alive in me. Maybe that's why Jesse needed to stay with me. And when it turned out to be longer than either of us expected, I didn't mind. I mean, I wasn't going to put him out after all he'd been through. He made my knees weak, he was so handsome and alone. But what can a dancer do with weak knees except to keep on dancing?

Which is what I did with Phillip when Mama braided my hair into coils of headache or raked my scalp until I thought I'd bleed, or when I couldn't help scratching the rash on my behind only to tear away the skin and bleed for real that time. I wasn't even having periods yet, but I was wearing all kinds of padded underwear and drinking goat's milk to heal my skin. All I wanted from Phillip was his tenderness, so that being a sickly colored girl wouldn't seem like the end of the world. I wasn't asking anything from Jesse, either. So when he called me, late as it was, I figured he could come right over. I had plenty of room. I wasn't asking for anything. For once, I could give something. We'd work on that dance, get ready for auditions, and-a one-two-three-four-five-six-seven-eight.

Wouldn't you know it'd be more complicated than that. Two days after Jesse's coming to stay with me, I came home to the smell of Lysol disinfectant and Ajax with ammonia. The apartment was as clean as a dime, and there was Jesse peeling potatoes at the sink, the dishes stacked up neat, the counter scrubbed to a shine, and the man had my apron on!

"I didn't expect you to clean the kitchen," I said.

"It's the least I could do. You're good enough to let me stay here."

"But Jesse," I said, looking around the kitchen, at the sunlight streaking through the rooms. "It's not only the kitchen, it's the whole place. You cleaned it all?"

"You've seen the bedroom?"

"Newspapers put away. Rug vacuumed. Clothes in the hamper. Even my dance tights folded neat. Do you do windows?" We both laughed.

"Just trying to be helpful."

"Your apartment must have been spotless," I said.

"I tried to keep it clean."

"Bet you didn't even have roaches, huh?"

"Squashed every one I saw. Twice I had the place exterminated myself when the landlord refused to do it."

"The whole building?"

"You kidding? Just our place."

"Two rooms?"

"Three."

"Me? I can live with roaches. They were here before I came, and they'll be here long after I'm gone."

"You have a nice place," said Jesse.

"You've made it nicer."

"I had something to work with. You coming to dance class? You ready for stretches, lunch?"

"Then off to the studio?"

"Sure."

"You're something else, Jesse."

I sat on the floor with my legs spread out and open, my tights lengthening to my flexed toes. Jesse sat opposite me. The soles of our feet pressed together. Tension increased. Every muscle of thigh, calf, ankle, and foot held firm. We gripped hands and leaned as far back as we could to stretch the back. Jesse pulled me forward. I pulled him forward. We pulled in a circle and pulled again until our torsos reached flat against the floor. We were both breathing heavily as if our bodies didn't quite match, and all the pulling and stretching was trying in vain to fit us together. I used to do this exercise with a girl my size. We had the same spread. With Jesse it was different. My pelvis and thighs stretched wider than before. The muscle tension in our swaying, stretching, pulling, give-and-take felt electric. Then I noticed the bulge in his tights. It grew larger into a fat ball he tried to hide but couldn't. How different men are! The same exercises don't apply. You have to consider differences in height, pelvis, groin. Then the grown-up Phillip came back to my mind in his dance of drugs, different from Jesse's stretches or his cleaning the kitchen, bedroom, and bath, or how I stretched close to the ground, pulling back and forth and not lifting my thighs, which was a way of hiding my

freckled ass when I was a kid or toe-tapping the air above a
man's pumping back now that I'm grown.

One night I heard Jesse crying. I got in the bed and held
him to my chest. Before I knew what was happening, I was
kissing the tears gathered at his lips, and when he realized
what was happening, he started kissing me. I felt something
crawl along my navel. The man's sex was in relevé all by
itself. We just stopped right there. Jesse calmed down, and I
told my jittery knees to get back in place, which they did,
but the flutter went all through me. I remembered the song
and Nina Simone's thick voice, and my trembling, improvising knees. Then it was my turn to sing, "He does not
know his beauty."

Why did he call me Rooms? What did he say about
Metro's name? Was Jesse going somewhere, too? They were
lovers, I understood that. But Jesse was still a man, the relevé
told me that much. While he slept, I touched myself all over
and found the spaces I could offer, all the rooms he could
visit.

The next morning he was fidgety. There was nothing
left to clean in the apartment. He did exercises, then paced
the floor. He searched my windows like a trapped bird and
wouldn't look me straight in the eyes. Ruella, girl, I told
myself, before you go off the deep end, you better find out
more. Don't stretch your heart to six-o'clock extension just
yet. You better find out something more. And Jesse's fear
told me, yes, there's a whole lot more here than Metro or
Phillip. But then again there's a lot more to me, too. Rooms,
somewhere.

We'd call the police again. Find out if they had gotten
anywhere on the case, if any one of us, Jesse included, knew
any more. Jesse picked up the phone and dialed nervously.
His voice cracked when he told the police who he was. I
stood next to him, my arms about his waist, his fingers
drumming the dial plate. I could hear the voice on the other
end of the line.

"Sergeant Porter speaking."

"This is Jesse Durand. I'm calling to see if, well, I'd like to know if, well, if you have any news on the Barthé murder on 12th Street?"

"You mean the attack by those teenagers?"

His fingers stopped drumming. "It was murder," he said.

"Oh, yeah. Detective Stone is looking into that one," the sergeant said. "I'll put him on."

We waited. Jesse looked at me. He looked back at the phone.

"Detective Stone here."

"I'm Jesse Durand."

"Yes, I have the Barthé file right before me. You're the roommate, right?"

"Yes."

"Listen. Could you come down here? I'd like to ask you a few more questions. It won't take long. Say tomorrow, about three?"

Jesse looked at me. I nodded and he nodded.

"Yes, we'll be there."

"We?" asked the detective.

You're never really prepared to just walk right into a precinct station. Inside, the glazed cinder-block walls and scuffed linoleum floors remind you of elementary school on the first day when you wanted to cry for Mama, or a hospital corridor without the smells of alcohol or medicine but you still have to get a needle, and it'll hurt. Jesse walked ahead of me up to the desk officer and stated his business. Our business. He directed us to an inside office where Detective Stone sat behind a small oak desk like a teacher and fingered a stack of files. I could see notes on yellow paper and the curled edges of some 8 x 10 glossy photographs which must have shown how they found Metro stabbed and dirty with leaves and street garbage and gravel. I didn't want to look too closely.

The detective rose from his desk and greeted Jesse. He turned to me with his eyebrows raised. "And you, Miss, Miss—"

"Ruella McPhee," I said. "I'm a friend of Jesse's."

Jesse relaxed a little, but I could see him tense up when the detective spoke to him again. I listened as carefully as I could.

"I'm sorry to have you come all the way down here, but there're some items we're not too clear about. We need more information."

"I'm sure I've already answered your questions," Jesse said, his words dancing on the edge of anger. "And you've still no lead on Metro's killers?"

"Metro?"

"I mean Barthé. Jon-Michael Barthé."

"Perhaps you can still help us. All we know so far is that he was severely beaten. Fatally wounded."

"You mean stabbed, don't you, Detective?"

"All right, stabbed."

"It's the truth."

"That happens often enough here when teenagers, you know, get it into their heads that—"

"They can beat up fags, you mean?" Jesse said. I could see the veins tighten at his neck. He opened and closed his empty fists. His eyes narrowed.

"Yes," said the detective. "That's right. But they may have just been fooling around, you know, showing off to each other. Kids do it all the time."

"But those kids killed him."

"We don't know anything for sure, now."

Jesse said nothing. He rolled his eyes at me.

"How long were you two living together on West 4th?"

"Only several months. We moved in last May. After college."

"And Barthé. Was he into drugs? Kinky sex? You know what I mean?"

"No, I don't know. Say what you mean, Detective. We were lovers, that's all, and long before we came to New York. A good thing, too, because this city will take everything you have."

"Did he have many friends in the city?"

"Only a few where he worked."

"He was a reporter, right?"

"Yes. At the *News.* Just starting out."

"I'll check with my sources there. Did he have other friends, I mean, other sexual partners?"

Jesse bit his lips and turned to me again. He looked back at the officer. "Yes."

"Anyone on a regular basis?"

"Me."

"When did you last see him?"

"I've given this information before, Detective. Why are you interrogating me?"

The detective seemed embarrassed. At least I thought so. He turned back to his file and shuffled several pages of notes through his hands. "I want to be sure I have all the facts, that's all. We have some reports from the neighbors. But you, Mr. Durand, did you see him earlier that evening?"

"Yes."

"At your apartment? On West 4th Street?"

"No. Actually, it was by the docks. Metro asked me to meet him there. He wanted to have a drink."

"May I ask what happened there?"

"We were just together. We had drinks. I don't even remember the name of the bar."

"And after?"

"I left him after an hour. I had a dance class. He said he would meet me later at home. He never made it back."

"What do you think happened?"

"That's what I'm here for, Detective. To find out."

"Look, don't get upset with me. Blood tests showed not only that he had had a lot to drink but that he'd taken tranquilizers."

"But what about the cause of death? The coroner's report? I saw the body. I saw how they cut him up."

"We're still investigating that."

"You don't really care. What's one more faggot dead? I'm glad Metro wasn't black. Then you'd forget about the whole thing. But Metro was a white boy, Detective. He had family."

The officer stood up from his desk. "We'll call you when we have something."

Jesse reached for my hand. "I'm not staying there anymore. I'm with Rooms."

"Rooms?"

That's when I cleared my throat, gave my teeth some air. I smiled and spoke my name with great precision. "Ru-el-la McPhee."

Jesse was already pulling me toward the door.

"Please leave your number with the desk officer, and I'll call you both if anything develops."

"If?" asked Jesse.

"As things develop," he said firmly and sat back down. It then occurred to me that he never shook Jesse's hand. Nor mine.

I gave my telephone number and address and left with Jesse. He walked ahead of me again through the tiled hallway, the scuffed linoleum echoing our steps. Outside a chill was rustling the trees. I held Jesse's hand, but he let go and put his hands in his pockets instead. At the corner of 7th Avenue he stopped, and I stopped, for the traffic going both ways fast. I held his hand, harder this time, until the veins showed through my skin.

We went into the IRT entrance, got tokens, and waited for the train. The smell of burning wires came through the tunnel and made me want to leave and take the bus. But there we were. We had paid our fare. We were trapped. The local howled in and I covered my ears. The bell rang. "Step in and watch the closing doors," said the motorman. In twenty minutes we were back at my place.

Lonny 7

ike I keep telling you. October is a bitch, a mean, red
bitch. And you still don't believe me. Shit, you got the red
leaves, you got early nightfall and twisted chilly mornings
freezing you back into bed. You got people in scarves and
caps tilted to the side like Hollywood detectives. You got
October. What more do you want? You want red leaves
clogging the sewers? You want legs and arms splayed out
like tree limbs after a storm? You really don't believe in
fall, huh, or how people can change too, just as fast? You
want all this? Then you're no better than that faggot who
wanted me.

He said his name was Metro. Just like that, he said it,
out of the blue. So I said, "Yeah." Nothing more. The way
he looked at me I could tell he was thinking he'd seen me
around and knew I'd seen him around, too, and after saying
hello just once he could come up to me a week later and tell
me his funny name.

I was on my way to meet Cuddles who had the smoke
this time. I had my mind on herb and didn't really see him
until he was close enough to speak. "Metro," he said. I
thought he was asking for directions. But he stuck out his
hand, 'cause it wasn't a place he was telling me, it was his
name. I felt a load on me from the moment he spoke. All I
said was "yeah." He didn't take the hint. He waited for more.
Maybe he was thinking the cat got my tongue and he wanted
it. I looked closer. He was about my height and build. Had
wavy hair, not stringy like mine. He looked like any regular

guy, except he spoke in a drawl straight out of *Gone with the Wind,* then changed back to a normal voice, like my voice changes sometimes, but not that bad. He said again his name was Metro. What could I do? He waited for me to tell him my name, but I never did. I finally said, "You know what you are?"

"Metro."

"Shit, man, you better get out of my face." And I left him standing there, looking like he just lost some money or came home to find his apartment broken into and his stereo and favorite record gone. With the wind. How do I know he even had a stereo? I don't know. He never invited me in to smoke dope or listen to records. Which is the only reason anyone would go with him. With a name like Metro, what would you expect?

I didn't expect nothing at all. The third time I seen him walking into the corner building, I knew he lived there. I wasn't meeting Cuddles that time. I didn't know why I was even in the neighborhood. You get used to meeting friends in the late afternoon and it gets to be routine. Metro was dressed in a suit, no jeans, no flannel plaid, no white under-shirt poking from inside the open collar. He looked like one of those Wall Street businessmen, he looked so square, so regular. He might have been somebody's husband or some-body's father even though he wasn't that old. You should know about fathers. They're the most important people to a kid trying to be a man, when everyone is out to get you or fix you into a can or a crate going six feet down.

My father built things. He was a carpenter mainly. He'd build things, take things apart, and build them again. But he was also an electrician, a house painter, a wallpaper hanger, a welder, a car mechanic, a plumber. All for money and for fixing up other people's houses. He could fix anything. A regular jack-of-all-trades. I remember he used to make toys for us at Christmas because he couldn't buy any. We was living in the Bronx then, and my father would load up his beat-up station wagon every morning and go off on the jobs people called him for. He owned his business. He was his own business. That's what Moms said to write in the blank beside "father's occupation" on school registration forms every September: "self-employed." I didn't even know what it meant, because my father never talked to us. He didn't tell us about who we were. I mean, as a family. And since I didn't know who I was aside from nothing or no one, I thought I could be anybody I damn well pleased.

"You ain't never had a chance, have you?" Moms said once.

"What are you talking about? I'm anybody I'm strong enough to be."

"And mean enough," she said, shaking her head like she did when my father died. He worked all the time and kept his feelings locked inside him until his heart burst open. The fucking load he must have been carrying. Shit, I coulda carried some of that load.

"You ain't never had a chance," Moms said again.

"I make my own chances. I'm self-employed."

Naw, Metro couldn't have been anybody's husband or father. You could tell by the way he walked and, if you listened close enough, by the way he talked. He had what you call opportunities. Maybe if you don't ever have kids you can build things for yourself. Do things. He just made the mistake of wanting to do me.

"You can come up to visit sometime, you know. Now that you know where I live."

"You mean me?"

"Sure. What's your name?"

"Lonny."

"I'm Metro."

"You told me before. Remember?"

"Yes. I thought you didn't remember. You didn't say anything."

"I didn't know what to say. Besides, where'd you get a name like that?"

"You'll see."

"Listen man, you trying to get wise or something?"

"Let's be friends, Lonny."

"I got to go now."

"Some other time, then?"

"Sure, man, sure."

"Call me Metro. I like that."

"Sure."

I got away and ran all the way to Cuddles' place. He wasn't even expecting me. But I was there just the same, leaning against the corner beam of the loading platform. It was about five feet off the ground so that the packing trucks could be loaded from the level of the storage and work areas. I could have been holding up the very corner of the building myself, or at least the sign saying Holsworth Meat and Poultry Packing, where you could actually see the sides of beef, the blood and fat making the loading-platform floor slippery and the whole place smell like rotten armpits.

Maybe it was the heat. Or just me, hot with my tangled nerves sizzling electric. All from talking with that guy Metro and running at breakneck speed to Cuddles' job like it was the only safe place. I was hot standing there thinking about Metro and hating myself for letting him talk like that to me. Shit, he talked like he knew who I was or who I could be. Like he could actually see into my corduroy jacket, his eyes like fingers in my clothes—touching me. You ever get that feeling talking to someone? Shit. I hated him for thinking he knew who I was and could come on to me like I was some bitch. He didn't know who he was messing with. Sure, I told him my name. We was just talking. Wouldn't you talk before you realized his eyes were fingers crawling all over you? I know you would, mostly because you'd think a guy wouldn't do that to another guy.

Later, you'd swear he hadn't touched you. Wouldn't you? You'd think that talking was all right. It was only some words between you, not hands. You'd think that as long as he didn't touch you it would be all right to speak. Long as neither of you was touching. It don't mean that you're one of them, just 'cause you say "Lonny," like I did. We was only talking, man. But when you realized his eyes were fingers taking hold, you'd hate him even more for pulling it off, undressing you right there with his eyes and laughing at your naked ass or shriveled-up cock. You'd be mad enough to kill him.

"You lying," Cuddles says when I tell him. "You lying, man."

"Naw, I ain't."

"Shit, man. Wait till I see Maxie and Lou."

"What for?"

"We oughta kick his ass."

"Look, Cuddles. Maybe we can just forget it, huh?"

"Naw, man. You one of us. What happens to you, happens to us. You forgetting the pledge."

"What pledge?" I ask after him, and he's dancing on the same short circuit I'm on.

When we catch up with Maxie and Lou, it's Cuddles doing the talking. "Man, we should celebrate," he yells, looking me over.

"Celebrate what?" I ask.

"Losing your cherry to a faggot, what else?" he says.

My face burns. "He didn't touch me, man."

"Aw, Lonny, we know you got a little bit," says Maxie grinning.

"Don't start no shit," says Lou.

"Maybe that's what I'm smelling," says Cuddles, moving up then back from me and flailing his arms like he's brushing me off.

"You mean the shit on *your* breath," I say, stepping up to him.

And Maxie jumps up and goes "Whoa," and Lou goes "Whoa," and I go "Whoa."

Cuddles backs off. "I'll fix your ass," he says. "Fix it real good."

"Aw, man, we been low too long now, let's ride high," says Maxie.

"Beer and smoke?" I ask.

"Yeah."

"Let's ride and fuck the night," adds Lou. He revs up

the cycle with Cuddles holding tighter to him than I ever held. At the first red light Cuddles turns to me, saying he'll fix me real good. I tell him where to put that shit.

Around midnight, after five trips to Burger King for fries and hot apple pies to ease the munchies, we get back to the garage in Chelsea. I'm high, yeah, I admit it. Feeling good. We stop cutting up with each other and just enjoy being so bloated we can barely move. We keep talking shit, though, like it's all we can say. But I still feel funny about meeting Metro earlier in the afternoon. A numbing tingle comes through my face like I'm getting high all over again or just burning slowly inside. Then I feel light again as if something is about to happen to ease the beer and marijuana out of me on a cool streak, and I'd lift off the garage floor, lift up from the street and glide out to 12th Street and Bleecker and on to West 4th, where I'd be sure to see him and we'd talk. Just talk. Maybe this time I would get to hear his stereo. Maybe he likes the same music I do. Maybe he really is like me or Maxie or Cuddles or Lou, just a little haywire.

But we leave the garage again and move in a group through the meat-packing section of West 12th and down toward Bleecker where men walk alone or in twos, passing us. Lou scowls. Cuddles sets his shoulders broad. We're a solid block, and tough. Them faggots is just maggots on rotting meat. They move away from us and off the sidewalk quick. Lou and Cuddles laugh, and I hardly know their voices. When I laugh too, just to be laughing, the chuckle comes out of some pit inside me, and the voice ain't mine, honest. Like the shit you don't know you carry around until it starts to stink.

Some guy up ahead is selling loose joints for a dollar. "All our joints loose," says Maxie, laughing and trying to unzip his pants. When we come up to him Maxie asks, "Got fifteen?"

"We'll get blasted to hell," I say. But no one answers. They all look like they know something I don't know.

Maxie asks for change of a twenty. I see Cuddles and

Lou sneak in close, so I move in close. The guy fumbles around in his pockets and gives me the joints to hold. As soon as he brings out a wad of bills it's a flurry of green and fists. Cuddles first, then Maxie. Lou, and me pounding hard on the upbeat.

"That's all the money I got," the guy whines. Cuddles pushes him away from us. The flash of metal makes the kid back right into Lou who feels his ass. Cuddles gets a feel, too. The guy's face goes red and his voice trembles, "Leave me alone. You got what you wanted."

"You oughta be glad we don't make you suck us off," Lou says, pushing him away. "Now get the fuck outta here."

The kid disappears down a side street. We count the new joints and money and move in close ranks like an army of our own, the baddest white boys out that night. Everyone else moves off the sidewalk as we approach, some we even push into the street, just close enough to a car to scare them clean out of their designer jeans and alligator shirts. The funniest shit is that some of them have on leather bomber jackets, and here we are doing the combat. We blow some of the cash at the liquor store off Sheridan Square.

On a vacant stoop near West 4th Street, we finish off the beer and the joints and divide up the rest of the money. Everything is sweet now. Sure we have our fights and fun and great highs. So what if they don't last long? Sure as shit and just as loud as the beer and smoke would let him, Cuddles goes, "Lonny, man, how's Beatrice these days?"

"Don't be bringing my Moms into your shit," I say.

"Keep it clean, guys," says Maxie.

"I was trying to keep it clean," Cuddles starts. "But the bitch had her period right when I was fucking her."

In a second I'm on him with fists and feet. He deserves no better. "We dancing this one, asshole."

"Yo, man, cool it," says Lou. He and Maxie pull me off Cuddles, but not until I land some good ones. Cuddles is too high to fight good. I could be faster myself, but what the hell.

"Aw man," Cuddles says, rolling to his side, sliding down the concrete stairs away from me. "I just wondered if she knew about your boyfriend. You know, the one you said lived around here."

"Whoa," says Maxie. "Lonny getting faggot pussy again? Keeping it all to himself?"

"It ain't true, man," I say.

"What ain't true?"

"This guy just told me his name, that's all. I didn't say nothing else. Nothing."

"Why he tell you his name then?"

" 'Cause he wanted to, that's why. You jealous, Cuddles?"

"Shit, man."

"He wanted to do something, I guess," I say.

"Of course he wanted to," says Maxie.

"He was trying to rap to me," I say, but I'm talking too much and can't stop. "Like I was some bitch."

"He touch you, man? He touch you?" Maxie asks.

"Shit," says Cuddles. "Faggots everywhere."

"I ain't no faggot," I say.

"He touch you, man?" asks Maxie.

"Like you touched that reefer kid back there?"

"That's different, Lonny. We was on top."

"Shit," says Cuddles. "Pass me another joint."

"Me too."

"Pass Lonny another joint. He cool."

"Thanks."

Hours pass. Or minutes that seem like hours. The streets are suddenly quiet and so are we. But that kind of quiet—sneaking up and banging like a fist on your face—makes you think something's about to happen and no laughing or getting high can stop it. What you do won't be all that strange, either, more like something you always thought about doing but never did. I hate that feeling. It makes me think that something's burning in me that I don't know about. And I've got to let it out or choke on the fumes.

Cuddles is the first to see him strolling down the street. He nudges me and Maxie. Maxie nudges Lou, who's half-asleep and stroking himself hard again.

"Aw, shit." My voice gives it away.

"That's him, ain't it?" asks Cuddles. "That's Lonny's faggot, ain't it?"

"I didn't say that," I say, but it's too late.

"He the one touch you?" asks Maxie.

"That's the one," says Cuddles.

"How do you know?"

"You told me," Cuddles says, but his voice also tells me something I can't get ahold of. They ease into the street and wait. I join just to be joining them. Metro approaches diz-zily, either drunk or high or plain out of it, but not as bad as the rest of us. Cuddles speaks up like he has it all worked out in his head.

"Hey, baby," he goes, in a slippery, chilly voice.

"Huh?" says Metro.

"Hey subway, baby," Cuddles goes again.

"The A train, right? I just took the A train," says Metro.

"We got another train for you, baby. A nice, easy ride."

I can't believe what Cuddles is saying. I try to hide my surprise by not looking at Metro, but they both scare me like I've never been scared before. It's something I can't get hold of or stop.

"Metro. Why do they call me Metro?" he goes, talking to himself all out of his head now. Does he even see these guys, hear them?

"Hey, baby," says Lou, getting close to him.

I stay where I am near the concrete steps.

"Oh, baby," says Maxie, joining in.

"They call me the underground man," says Metro, his words slurring. "You wanna know why? I'll tell you why." His eyes dart to all of us, locking us in a space he carries inside for someone to fill. Then he sees me for the first time. He stops, jaws open, eyes wide. "Is that you, Lonny?"

I say nothing. The guys are quiet, too.

"You wanna know why, Lonny? Cause I get down under. Underground. Metro. Get it?" Then he laughs a high, faggoty laugh. And I don't know him anymore. He stops suddenly. No one else is laughing. He feels something's wrong. He looks straight at me, then at the others now tight around him.

"Lonny, what's going on? Who are these guys?"

Cuddles touches him, his hand gliding down Metro's open shirt. Metro's eyes get round.

"Lonny, I don't know these guys."

"That's all right," says Maxie. "We're Lonny's friends. Ain't that right, Lonny?"

I say nothing. Lou kicks me square in the shins. "Yeah," I say. "Yeah." But nothing more.

"And when Lonny tells us you go under, man, you give it up nice and easy, don't you?" says Cuddles.

Metro reaches into his pockets and pulls out a raggedy leather wallet. "I don't have much money." He shows the wallet around so we see the single ten-spot inside. "That's all there is. You want it? It's all I have."

"No, baby," says Cuddles. "Keep your money. Right, fellahs?"

"Right."

Metro looks worried. "My watch? I don't have anything else. Nothing, honest. You can check if you want."

"We don't want your watch," says Lou. His hand falls to Metro's ass, feeling it. Then to the front, gathering Metro's balls into a hump and slowly releasing them.

"Lonny says you been after him."

"After him? I don't understand. What are they saying, Lonny?"

I don't say nothing, but I want to say something. When I step closer, I feel metal pointing in my side, a blade tearing my shirt. Cold on my skin.

"Yeah," I say. "You been after me."

Cuddles steps up. "You wanted to suck his cock? Take it up the ass?"

"Hold it, Cuddles," I say.

"Naw, you hold it," says Maxie. "You could be like that too, for all we know. Ain't that right, fellahs?"

"Shit, man. You tell him, Cuddles. Tell him he's crazy to think that. You seen me with that girl."

"Naw, man. You show us," Cuddles says.

They hustle me and Metro to an alley near the abandoned building and stoop. Maxie and Lou hold Metro by the armpits. Cuddles twists my arm behind my back, and from his open breath I know he's grinning ear to ear. "Aw, man," he whispers to me. "We just having fun. Gonna shake him up a little."

"What about me?"

Cuddles says nothing more. He looks at the others.

Maxie pushes Metro to the ground. The alley carries his voice. "You wanted to suck him, huh? Well, suck him."

Cuddles unzips my pants.

"I didn't touch you, Lonny. I never touched you."

"You lying, subway man," says Cuddles.

"Ask him," says Metro. "Did I touch you, Lonny? Ever? You can tell them. Please, Lonny. I never touched you."

All eyes are on me now, and even in the dark I can see the glimmer of Metro's eyes looking up from the ground. From the sound of his voice I can tell he's about to cry. Suddenly, the click of knives: Lou's and Maxie's. Metro faces away from them and can't see. I see them, but I say nothing. Cuddles twists my arm further. The pain grabs my voice. His blade against my skin. "I told you I'd get back at you, shithead."

Pain all in me. Metro jerks forward. "Ouch," he says feeling a blade, too. Then Metro's mouth in my pants. Lips cold on my cock. Then warmer. Smoother. Teeth, saliva, gums. I can't say nothing, even if I want to.

It don't take me long. I open my eyes. Metro's head is still pumping at my limp cock, but his pants are down in the back, and Lou is fucking him in the ass. Lou gets up quickly, zips up his pants. Maxie moves to take his place. I move out of Metro's mouth, open in a frown this time or a cry. Maxie wets his cock and sticks it in. Cuddles pumps Metro's face where I was. Metro gags. Cuddles slaps his head back to his cock, and I hear another slap. This one against Metro's ass, and Lou and Maxie slap his ass while Maxie fucks him. Lou has the knife at Metro's back and hips. He traces the shape of his body with the blade. Metro winces. "Keep still, you bastard. Keep still," Lou says.

I try to make it to the street, but Cuddles yanks me back. He hands me a knife and I hold it, looking meaner than I am. You ain't never had a chance, I'm thinking and realizing it's for Metro, not for me. Cuddles finishes and pulls out of Metro's dripping mouth. His fist lands against Metro's jaw, slamming it shut. I hear the crack of bone and a weak cry. The next thing I know, Maxie, still pumping Metro's ass and slapping the cheeks with the blade broadside, draws blood, and once he finishes he shoots the blade in, then gets up quick, pulling the knife after him. Lou's hand follows. Then a flash of metal and fists.

"Shit, man. Hold it," I yell. "I thought we was only gonna fuck him. What the hell you guys doing?"

"Fucking him good," says Lou.

"Stop. For God's sake, stop."

But they don't stop.

"Oh my God. Oh my fucking God." It's all I can say, damn it. And I hear my name.

"Lonny?"

"Oh my God."

"Lonny?" Metro's voice is weak, his words slurring on wet red leaves. "Help me."

Lou and Maxie jump together. "Let's get the fuck outta here."

"Yeah," says Cuddles. He kicks Metro back to the ground where his arms and legs spread like the gray limbs of a tree.

"Oh my fucking God." I keep saying it, crying it. But

it's too late. The guys scatter into the street like roaches surprised by light. Running. They're running. I look back at Metro and he rolls toward me. His still eyes cut me like a blade. "Never touched you," the eyes say. "Never touched you."

I hold my breath until my ears start to pound. I hold my head. I run, stop, run again. The knife drops somewhere. I run again. Don't know where the fuck I'm going, just getting the hell out of there. Don't see anybody on the street and not for the rest of the night. Not Lou, not Cuddles. Not anybody else at all.

October is red, man. Mean and red. Nobody came back there but me, see. And Metro was gone by then. Somebody had raked the leaves into a clean pile. I ran through it and scattered the leaves again. Once you get leaves and shit sticking all on you, you can never get them off. And when you start hearing the scratchy, hurt voices coming from them, the leaves I mean, not patches of skin or a body cut with knives, or a palm of broken fingers, you'll start talking back, like I do. You stop hanging out at the meat-packing warehouses on West 12th or walking the loading platform mushy with animal fat and slime where your sneaks slip—not Adidas, but cheaper ones just as good.

When I found Cuddles and told him about the talking red leaves, he said to get the fuck away from him, stop coming around if I was gonna talk crazy and dance out of fear like a punk. But I wasn't dancing. My feet was trying to hold steady on the loading platform, but my sneaks wouldn't let me. You ever hear the scratchy voices of leaves? You ever try to hold steady on slippery ground?

They had the body marked out in chalk on the ground behind some blue sawhorses that said "Police Line—Do Not Cross." It was right where we left him. I saw it glowing. "Here's Metro," I told myself. Here's anybody, even me. A chalk outline and nothing inside. A fat white line of head, arms, body, and legs. A body curled into a heap to hold itself. Like a leaf or a dead bird, something dropped out of the sky or from a guy's stretched-out hand. It was amazing. But it was also the figure of somebody. A man. Any man. So I walked around the outline, seeing it from different angles. How funny to see something that fixed, protected from people or from falling leaves or from the slimy drippings from sides of beef. The outline wasn't Metro. It was somebody like me.

Once I saw the chalk figure I couldn't get enough of it. I kept coming back and walking slower and slower around it, measuring how far it was from the police barricade and from where I stood looking down at it, sprawled where we left him. But I figured out a way to keep looking at it and not step in the garbage scattered nearby. You know, leaves, rags, torn newspapers, bits of dog hair, blood maybe, and lots more leaves. I went three steps this way and three steps that way, keeping the chalk outline in sight and missing the garbage and dogshit. One-two-three, one-two-three. Up-two-three, down-two-three. When I saw one of the neighbors watching from a window, I cut out of there. By then I knew what I had to do.

I came back that night. The chalk shape was glowing like crushed jewels under the streetlights. I took off my shirt and pants and didn't even feel cold. I crossed the barricade and sat inside the chalk. The glow was on me now. It was me. I lay down in the shape of the dead man, fitting my head, arms, and legs in place. I was warm all over.

The police came and got me up. Their voices were soft and mine was soft. They pulled a white jacket over me like some old lady's shawl. I shrugged a little to get it off, but my arms wouldn't move. When I looked for my hands, I couldn't find them. The police didn't ask many questions, and I didn't say nothing the whole time. At the precinct, a doctor talked to me real quiet-like and said the leaves would go away forever if I told him everything that happened to the dead man and to me. But they didn't call him Metro, they called him some other name with an accent in it. A name I didn't even know. I asked the doctor again about the red leaves. He promised they would go away. "What about the blood?" I asked. "Will I step in the blood?"

"Not if you come clean," he said.

"What about my sneaks?" I asked him. "Will they get dirty?"

PART TWO

Ruella

I wasn't even out of my building yet, and there I was rushing to a job. Then it hit me how I hated taking the subway. I hated all the darkness and the smell of burning electricity and the speed rattling loud at my head. I didn't want to be that close to all those people. Falling into step with folks I didn't even know. Everybody going somewhere. Fast-stepping when the music was only a waltz. Where was Fred Astaire when you needed him?

At home it was a different kind of dance, Jesse cleaning the apartment like a maid gone mad, washing each dish as soon as it got dirty, sweeping crumbs from the kitchen floor. He was about to drive me crazy. I couldn't even throw my leotards onto the bed anymore, without him coming up behind me and folding them neat. I'm glad I didn't smoke, or he'd have been forever emptying the ashtrays. And wouldn't you know, when he wasn't cleaning or exercising or straightening up, he sat perched like a trapped bird searching my windows, which were clean now on both sides, thanks to him. What that man wouldn't have done.

I teased him to get his sense of humor back. I tried out something new, a *pas de deux* with sounds and steps. "Eh-yah?"

"Caroom-boom clack," he answered.

"Eh-yah."

"Caroom-boom clack."

I grabbed his hands and pulled him around and around and we were kids again playing Ring-Around-the-Rosy and Little Sally Walker. I spun and he spun and we all fell down. The soles of our feet came together. We stretched long, low, and wide from the hips, then sat up like chocolate Buddhas, contracting stomach and chest in and out, in and out, two, three. I moved right into a lotus position he couldn't do. I had him then. But he went off to the kitchen and started making dinner.

Soon I was sitting at the prettiest table. A vase of yellow freesias, red paper napkins, and Aunt Lois's glass salad bowl dug out from a closet somewhere. Well, a man like that was a find. I hugged him good and he hugged me. This time I had to tell him about Phillip. Clear things up before I lost my way. Ruella, girl, how do you always get tangled up in these things?

"Jesse, you're just like my brother."

"What's wrong with that?"

"I already have a brother. His name is Phillip."

"So do I, only his name is Charlie and we can't stand each other."

"Well, Phillip and I have had our differences," I said, trying to ease up on what was really on my mind. "He's in jail now, busted for dealing in heroin."

"Oh," said Jesse with a scared look, like he'd got mixed up in some other mess.

"I'm not into drugs," I said. "Not me, chile. And I'm only bringing him up to say, well, I have a brother, Jesse. What I don't have is a lover." And there I sat with my mouth hanging open, like the words just fell out on their own. Jesse looked at me and didn't say a thing. So I grinned and pulled my mouth in shut. Jesse chuckled, laughed. Then I started laughing for no reason at all, just seeing him laugh which made me laugh some more. Then we stopped. Just like that. I figured I could give him something Metro didn't have. If he wanted to call me Rooms, well, he should know what spaces I really had. How much there really was in me. I never said I was pretty. But I have my good points.

That night I climbed right on top of him. I rocked back

and forth, smooth and easy. Jesse didn't move. His eyes stayed wide open on the ceiling as if his powers of concentration could lift it right off. Then I rolled off him, pretending that all I wanted was to tickle him some, make him laugh again. Truth is, I felt silly. Real dumb. I tried to turn it into a game. Girl, I told myself, all embarrassed and blushing in the silent way colored girls blush, whatever did you expect to happen? One relevé doesn't make a dance. He has to move with you. Rhythm isn't a one-person thing.

My own advice didn't help. I felt as small as a roach caught on its back, feet treading and tapping the air, eyes and antenna searching every which way and trying not to think about myself because I'd break down and cry, I was so embarrassed. Jesse squeezed my hand. Held it, like Phillip used to do. But Mama wasn't there combing my hair, and the rash on my behind had long since gone, and the heat in me was just plain shame that my need could show up naked like that when you had to be cool about it. How could I have made Jesse know what he could have done for me? I was afraid he already knew.

"It's my fault," I said. "I'm sorry."

"No, Rooms, it's mine."

"Look, Jesse, we don't have to, I mean, there's no pressure on you or anything. Shoot, I can't even talk right. Here I am falling for you, you handsome thing, you. And, well, I'm not a pretty woman."

"Who said? I sure didn't," he said.

Well, I shut up just as quick. "There you go, Jesse. All charm and grace."

"I'm being honest with you, Rooms."

"Then call me Ruella, my real name."

"Ruella."

I took a deep breath. "Don't call me Rooms. Not unless you mean to come through the door." I felt much better saying it.

"Ruella, Ruella," Jesse said. "Pretty Ruella."

"Don't mess with me, Jesse. Don't play with me. Not now, please, not now."

"We danced."

"And we've been improvising ever since, huh? I need something more, Jesse. Something more than dancing. I can always dance solo."

"I don't want to hurt you, Rooms."

"Ruella."

"Ruella, I don't want to hurt you, ever."

"I'm not that fragile, Jesse."

"But I am," he said. He pulled back the covers and got out of bed.

"Where're you going?"

"I am just that fragile."

"Can't you put Metro out of your mind for a minute?"

"Like you've put Phillip out of yours?"

"That's not fair, he's in jail."

"So am I."

That shut me up. Jesse started dressing in the dark. I turned on the light and moved so he couldn't see me blink back the tears. "Where are you going?" I asked, but he gathered his clothes in one sweep and opened the bedroom door.

"Maybe I shouldn't have come here."

"No, Jesse. Don't say that."

"I'll go. I'm sorry if things got out of hand."

"Please stay, Jesse."

"I'll call you later."

The front door eased shut behind him. His fast feet hit the stairs. I was too ashamed of myself to look after him or say anything more. But all night I couldn't sleep for Jesse, then Phillip, then Jesse again crowding my mind, a rushing D train in my head.

There was only one thing to do. Ride out to see Phillip. I called in sick the next morning and went to Port Authority for the early bus going upstate. Comstock Prison is about two hundred miles north. Maybe Phillip could help me figure this one out. Ruella, girl, you really messed up this time.

★ ★ ★

The first year he was in I wrote and asked about his room. "What room, Lil' Sis? This ain't no hotel, it's a goddamn prison." He described the place. "It's a cell, a goddamn 10 x 12 cell and nothing but bars and electronic locks and feet scuffling on the grated ceiling walk that separates the floors and reminds you that you're never alone."

After looking at the huge tan-brick building fenced in on all sides and counting row after row of bars on windows I had to say, you're right, Phillip; no rooms. Cells. C-e-l-l-s. "You still want me for your hero, Lil' Sis?" he wrote. "Being heroic and black ain't easy. 'Specially if you a man. Ain't nothing here but men. Black men, Puerto Rican men, even one or two white boys. You'll see what I mean when you come next Visiting Day. I missed you the last time."

I didn't write him back. I didn't visit. Truth is, until now I was scared.

The visitors' room crowded quickly with women, mostly those from the same bus I took which ran from the Greyhound Terminal in Saratoga to the prison grounds several miles away. They were weary women. Some brought their children along. Others looked like young marrieds and were not much older than me. The younger ones wore tight blue jeans and loose, open tops. The mothers, perhaps, or wives of older inmates wore shawls or closed sweaters. Everyone was chattering and crowding into their assigned booths behind a glass wall.

Several prisoners entered first, and I was afraid Phillip would miss me or just not come. But sooner than I knew he appeared just inside the door and came toward my booth. He didn't seem to recognize me. He moved mechanically, with the same indifference and routine of the guards motioning him to the booth, which was more like a cubicle than a desk, with glass walls for visiting. Perhaps Phillip was expecting the public defender or one of his drug cronies who didn't get caught. Maybe even someone from the local community concerned about prison conditions. Maybe a preacher looking for converts. Anyone with promises to offer. Anyone but me.

Phillip was taller now and much larger than the thin, nervous man I saw three years ago. His hair was shorter and his eyes were larger than I remembered. Three years ago he had returned home fresh from the West Coast with money and time to burn and Los Angeles on the brain. His California road map had hypodermic needles and burnt spoons between the folds. New Jersey was nothing after L.A., and there I was living with Aunt Lois since Mama died. I was just out of high school and trotting off to dance class in Manhattan twice a week. I didn't know anything about Hollywood, or the Pacific Coast Drive, or having the good times he talked about and missed. Aunt Lois just wanted him to get a decent job. She wanted him to be safe. "For his own good," she told me. But she also wanted me safe away from him. I wanted to hear all about the surf and film studios and freeways giving you the itch to move, not his cheap hotels and sidewalk hits or running out of money and peddling anything on two feet.

But the Phillip straining to see me and almost walking past my booth was a paler Phillip than I remembered. I grinned and waved from my seat. His eyes sparkled for a moment like he was still figuring out who I was. I grinned again and he knew me. His eyes lowered away from me and back toward the door he had come from. I smiled again and lifted the telephone to speak. He sat down reluctantly. I had to knock on the glass to get him to pick up the receiver and talk.

"You never came before," Phillip said. His voice was different. I watched him closely. He spoke slowly, each word weighing the last. "You never came before."

"I couldn't Phillip. I wanted to. I couldn't." I tried to smile.

"It wasn't Aunt Lois those times before, was it? You ain't even living there no more."

I said nothing.

"My letters came back," he continued. "Addressee unknown. No forwarding address. I can't blame you for cutting out on Aunt Lois. But did you have to cut out on me too?"

"She knew where I was. She even encouraged me to leave. I was old enough, Phillip."

"And did she keep you from visiting me before or hide my letters from you after a while? But you old enough, you said it yourself."

"That's why I'm here now. I couldn't bring myself to visit before. You were so strange, so different. I wasn't ready to see you, Phillip."

"What you mean, ready? I'm your brother. The closest kin you got. And they killing me in here."

"I'm sorry." I couldn't say anything more. I looked at him but he looked above me, not at me. He must have been watching the guard, the clock, the other prisoners, their visitors and animated conversation, the exchange of hopeful looks, I didn't know. If I could have just touched him then, felt the texture of his face and known that mine had the same toughness of character, I'd have come back again and again just to help him and help myself be strong. I had to bite my lip to stop my eyes from filling up. I brushed them dry, still looking at him. Next to me, a woman pressed her lips to the glass, leaving the print of her lipstick. I turned back to Phillip and the glass between us. I tried to find something to say.

"Truth is, Phillip, I've got to touch base with you. I don't really know what to say. You let me down. You were the only man who made me feel special, like I was a princess or someone important. Like I was even beautiful and deserved somebody's good attention. You were my hope after Mama died. I wanted to go places, do things, dance on every stage that would have me. And I thought you could help me do that."

Phillip watched me more closely than I wanted him to. "You couldn't face it, could you? And I can't really blame you for not facing it," he said.

"What, Phillip?"

"That I was just ordinary. Not the black prince every brown girl is waiting for. No dragon-slayer, not even a good pimp. Just the no-count nigger Aunt Lois always complained about."

"Forget about Aunt Lois. It's me I'm talking about."

"And me, Lil' Sis. You think I ain't worried about me? And brothers like me? Not just in this dump, baby. All over."

"I don't understand you."

"You still a kid. You see all these black men in here? This ain't just the colored section of the joint. This is it. All these niggers and nothing but niggers. This is where they put us when we don't dance to they music no more."

"But I was waiting, Phillip, I waited for that charm and magic. I waited while you were in California. I knew you'd get somewhere and send for me. I'd bring my toe shoes and leotards. Everything. But you got messed up in drugs and white folks. When you came back you had forgotten all about me. All you wanted was to get high and run the streets, so I figured I'd have to get where I wanted on my own. I didn't want to know about your deals in Harlem or your getting busted and sent here. Phillip, I wanted to dance and be whoever I could be dancing. And now, Phillip, if I can tell you, I got myself mixed up in something I don't understand. Something I can't get right. I'm through being someone else's dream or someone's sweet baby doll. Somebody's room or Lil' Sis or whatever you all need. You know what I mean?"

"No. I don't get you."

"I'm not down on men, Phillip. But something's happening to me that has to do with you, somehow. I don't understand it all myself."

"You must be mixed up with some man. You pregnant?"

"No. But you're right about the man. I'm with someone now. A friend needed a place to stay, real bad. I let him come to my place. He's a dancer like me. We're auditioning for the same company."

"You going together?"

"Sort of."

"What's he like?"

"He reminds me of you. I mean, we act together like you and I used to. We're close. We tell each other things and, well, he's not like other guys I've known. That's all I can say right now. But you'll meet him. I want you to."

"He don't know you got people here, huh?"

"He does now. I'll bring him along next time. I'll come to see you again, I promise."

"He fucking you?"

"Don't say it like that, Phillip. We're just starting out. We're taking our time. He's nice, intelligent. He's been to college."

"You happy?"

"I think so."

"I want you to be happy. I want to think about you being happy." Phillip looked at the other visitors and the other prisoners. He watched another prisoner talking to a woman. He watched intently, almost with caution.

"You'll be out soon," I told him. "What about parole? A couple of months? A year?"

"That's if I can hold on. Keep my temper even. Not let these motherfuckers mess with me. They do that, you know. The guards. Soon as you're close to parole they try to fuck with you so you start fighting them or cut somebody up and shit. Then you get more years in the joint."

"I don't understand what's happened to you. You wanted to be a lawyer once. You still read?"

"All the time. I got lots of time."

"Then hold out just a little longer. I'll get a larger apartment. You'll have a place to stay. I'll talk to my boss at the office about a job. Something. Anything. Too bad you're not a dancer."

"They all faggots anyway."

"Not all of them. And besides, they say the same thing about prisoners."

"Shit." The sudden look on his face shut me up real quick. His eyes lowered and all the determination there, which would have made him strong against the guards or other prisoners or those months until parole, was fading. I was more afraid for him then than for myself. His frustration might never get him out of there.

"I'm sorry I said that, Phillip. I didn't mean it like it sounded."

"That's all right."

"Listen, I'll be back in two weeks. I'll bring Jesse. That's his name. Jesse Durand. I told him about you. You were the most important man in my life. I didn't even know Daddy. You did. And you were him for me. And you were yourself. You're still important to me, Phillip."

Phillip smiled, but his eyes were distant. "Sure," he said. But his eyes searched around him on the prisoner's side of the glass.

"Here, I've brought you cigarettes and a book. I'll bring more, and you'll meet Jesse. You'll like him."

"I hope I'm not here. They're transferring me to Rikers since I'm so close to parole. You'll come visit then? It's closer than riding all the way up here."

"Yes, for sure."

"They think I'll have a better chance getting into some prerelease counseling program. That way it'll be easier to get work on the outside. I'll have a better chance for parole, too."

"You'll be out soon after that?"

"Soon. You check with Rikers. The transfer should come in a few days. You'll really come see me?"

"Yes, Phillip."

"I'll be looking for you."

Somewhere behind me a bell rang. The guard by the door blew a whistle and people began leaving the room. I looked at Phillip again and hung the receiver back on its hook. Phillip didn't get up right away, like he was waiting for something else. Another prisoner came up to him and patted him on the shoulder, almost leading him away. Phillip waved to me and smiled at the other prisoner. He spoke soundlessly to me again, his lips forming the word "soon" his finger pointing at me. And before I knew it, he was gone. When I turned around, I saw I was the last visitor to leave.

I boarded the bus waiting beyond the gates to the building. In Saratoga Springs I changed buses for New York City. I kept thinking of Phillip. He had smiled at me. He had smiled at the other prisoner. I had seen the difference in those smiles before.

By the time I got home it was late at night. The apartment felt empty. No use doing stretching exercises or yoga as tired as I was, so I went right to sleep. For once, the emptiness of the apartment was soothing. Jesse didn't come back the next morning, and I got to the office early enough to sort the mail. From the thirty-fifth floor I could see people scurrying inside before nine o'clock. And then I remembered that this building was a mere rectangle of cinder block, with the same squared windows one can see everywhere in New York City or in Comstock State Prison for that matter. Small difference between apartment windows with accordion gates and prison windows filled with metal slats for ventilation. Sunlight never had it so hard. I telephoned my apartment. No answer—Jesse hadn't returned. At noon, I went home for the day.

As soon as I entered the apartment I knew that Jesse had been there. Why hadn't he answered the telephone when I called? His signs were everywhere: dishes washed and put away, sofa pillows fluffed and propped into place. Cleanliness all over again and here I was messing it up. Then I noticed scraps of paper with phone numbers on the kitchen counter top.

I had a salad for lunch and packed my leotards and dance tights for class. Jesse would be there and we'd dance, letting the movement of our separate bodies work out the tension between us. Maybe. If we didn't dance together we'd at least have shared the same space. I'd have to work hard to make up for missing class the day before, but all I could think about during the stretching warm-ups, the triplets and leaps across the floor, the Graham contractions and Wideman extensions, was that Jesse wasn't there filling space with his arms and legs and gyrating torso or watching me watch him. It wasn't like him to miss class this close to audition date. During the ten-minute break before we worked in pairs for combinations across the floor, I asked among the other dancers. No one had seen him.

I caught the subway alone and climbed the stairs to my apartment, more tired than ever. But I couldn't stop thinking about Jesse. And Phillip. If Jesse came back—he must come back—they could meet. Maybe tonight after the bars closed, Jesse and I could talk. Maybe after dinner and exercises. Maybe, maybe. We wouldn't have to make love, just hold each other. I promised this time. The wallet papers on the counter top drew me away from the floor exercises and yoga. I flipped through the business cards, the coupons for reductions on food and dance tights, someone's telephone number with instructions to call only after 7:00 P.M. Then a tongue of envelope with its glue dried and cracking: West Street, Pier 52.

Just then the phone rang. A white man's voice. "Mr. Durand, please. Detective Stone here."

"No," I said in my best receptionist voice and holding the tongue of envelope with the pier address. "He isn't in. May I take a message?"

"Do you know where he is? You know if I can reach him someplace?"

"No, I'm sorry, Detective. This is Ruella. May I help you? Is this about the Barthé case?" I fingered the tongue of envelope again, the dry glue flaking off on my fingers, and I wasn't even biting my nails.

"Have him call me as soon as he gets in, please. We have a suspect. Someone found in the area. They say he was walking in circles. Lying on the ground nude. The neighbors called us right away."

"Walking in circles?"

"Yes. Right on the street where they attacked him."

"Jesse?"

"No, Barthé, Miss McPhee."

"I'm sorry. I'm a little off today. I'll tell Jesse to call you as soon as he gets in."

"I hope so. Good-bye, Miss McPhee."

"Ruella."

"Yes, Ruella. Good-bye."

He hung up and I read the envelope again. Then in careful folds, one atop the other, I put it by the phone and went to bed.

The next morning the regular secretary couldn't come in, so I had to work all day. I missed dance class again but went there to ask again if Jesse had been there. No one had seen him. The company instructor was a little worried. By this time he knew we were friends and told me Jesse had to show more dedication if he wanted to join the company. "More discipline, too," he said.

"And me? What about me?" I asked.

"I think I can use you both. We'll see at the auditions."

From the hallway of my building I heard my telephone ring and I bounded up the stairs. After fumbling with my keys I answered what was sure to be the last ring. Detective Stone again. His voice was decisive, but he was worried that Jesse still wasn't there.

"You don't think he's gone off looking for those guys?"

"I don't know. I hadn't thought about it, really."

"Well, it's no use. We got them. All of them."

"Thank God, Officer."

"You'll have him call me right away?"

"Yes. Yes, right away." I eased the receiver back onto the phone. Where was Jesse? Where had he been for two days? Ours was just a little fight, I thought. Not serious enough for him to be gone so long without word. And now good news: a chance to join the company and the arrest of the kids who attacked Metro. But where was Jesse? I remembered then the pile of wallet papers and the tongue of

envelope with his handwriting folded neatly and placed—
where? I looked frantically. The dresser drawer? The cabinet?
The telephone? Yes. There. West Street, Pier 52. I tossed the
slip of paper into my bag and headed for the IRT. The tights
made my legs heavy under my jeans. I prayed I could find
him.

Her hands kept sticking to me. Pulling on me. Holding fast. I needed to go somewhere, anywhere, quick. I rode the subway most of the night for as far as I could go on a single token. I'd give back to the trains the constant roaring in my chest. I wanted tunnels and lights and the grimy arms of travel. From 86th Street and Broadway, I took the downtown #1 IRT to Times Square, then the SS to Grand Central Station, walked through the underground passage to the Lexington Line and rode the #4 express to 14th Street, changed for the LL train over to the West Side at 8th Avenue, and there took the IND AA *caroom-boom-clack, caroom-boom-clack, caroom* to the E downtown at West 4th Street, switched to the uptown F train and changed at 42nd Street for the #7 Flushing, then uptown again on the Lexington #5 this time and changed at 59th Street for the BMT N train over again to the West Side, and the #1 local all the way to 125th Street, where the tracks come out of the ground and stand high above the streets and lights and noise.

I changed back to the downtown train and this time stood at the front-car window and watched the underground lights zoom in and flash by all through the dark and abandoned stations. I remembered Ruella's voice and Metro's voice clanging inside me. I sat alone in another car as the lights went off and on and off again. I changed trains at 34th Street, Penn Station, and stalked the platform, ready to jump onto the tracks, but there was garbage and water and the quick tarantella of rats. I got back on the train, a #2 smelling of electrical wires and rusty wheels. I could have traveled all night for just one fare going *caroom-boom-clack, caroom* nonstop until I was back at 14th Street. I left the subway and walked east. Three blocks later I found myself at the door to the Paradise Baths.

Metro had been there once and told me about it, all seven floors. Maybe being there would bring me closer to him, now that I was also a wanderer with no place to go. But would I have enough sense to stop myself from jumping from the roof of a thirty-story apartment building or kissing the blades of angry knives? I was running faster now, faster than a rat between subway tracks. Running away from Ruella who was a refuge no longer, not Rooms anymore, running from the Village to the Upper West Side and back again, running from downtown backroom bookstores where you can get a blowjob from other wanderers watching the same skin flick play out in private booths or private minds for twenty-five cents a reel. Or dingy and crowded baths where men wait in 4 × 8 cubicles, a single red bulb dimming on their supine bodies, ass up for fucking, balls up for sucking, and anonymous hands feeling you up or leading you into cellulite thighs. But this establishment, seven floors and only a subway ride away at the edge of Chelsea and the Village, is different. You have a choice of rooms.

Inside, there was a line at the reception desk and overhead signs offering discounts:

Locker Free to any Former P.O.W.

1/2 Price for Veterans.

Anyone in Uniform—Military or Police—A Free Room!

I couldn't afford a room so I took a locker. I signed the register "Jess B. Kind," checked my valuables, and went in.

One flight up, people were changing into towels or from towels to clothes. I looked for my locker, number 98, and kept bumping into mirrors.

"What number you got?" said a voice from somewhere. Then behind me. "What number?"

"Ninety-eight."

"Well, can't you see that the numbers go in order—"

"I'm sorry."

"Ninety-eight's over there. The sign says lockers 54 to 86, 87 to 112. See it to your right?"

I did, but once I found the locker I couldn't get it open. The key stuck and I tried the latch. That too wouldn't budge. Then the same voice came back, out of nowhere. "What's the matter? Can't get it open?"

He was a tall, heavy-set black man with large popeyes. His gray hair extended into sideburns and a thin gray beard. His belly protruded over the rolled edge of the towel stretched about his waist. "Here, let me try," he said, taking my key out and pounding the area around the latch. "Sometimes these things stick," he said. "You don't act like you been here before."

"No, I haven't. A friend told me about this place."

"So it's your first time?"

"Yes."

"Well, welcome to Paradise. All seven greasy floors of it."

"Why do you say that?"

"Because it's shit. The same ol' shit. I been coming here every Wednesday night for the discounts, you know, and it's always same ol' shit."

"Always?"

"Always. When you get undressed I'll show you around."

"You don't mind?"

"I been on all the floors at least twice already since eight o'clock. I'll show you around. My name's Clement. You can call me Clementine. I'm real, darling."

"I'm Jesse. You can call me Jesse."

"You sure look good, Jesse. Bet you got good meat, too."

"Now wait a minute, I just got here."

"Just warming you up, that's all. You can give it up any way you like. That's all I'm trying to say. There are no rules here. And tonight there's some real hungry numbers here, honey. I don't know why your lover even let you out."

"I don't have a lover. Not anymore."

"Lucky for me. I mean, how long were you together?"

"Two years."

"Honey, you complaining? That's a record in Manhattan. I've had me four lovers. One for every century I lived through, before I forgot how to count. I'm old as sin and just as fun. But I can still put them out when I want to. They don't leave me. What about you?"

"He was killed."

Clementine's eyes widened, then looked away. "Sorry."

"It's O.K. I don't think about it much anymore," I lied. "I want to have a good time tonight."

"Then let old Clementine show you around. I can speak Spanish, you know. French too, and some Italian. I'm a woman of many tongues."

"I bet you are."

"I'd sure like to put one in you. Get us real tongue-tied."

"I'm not available."

"You ain't no snow queen, is you? I like all types myself."

"Snow queen?"

"Into white boys, darling. A preference for the Nordic breed. You know, the Ice Age and northern Europe. I used to give concerts there. In Europe, when I was a singer. Now I just give voice lessons. You might say I've retired from the stage."

"I'm a dancer."

"And you ain't been to Paradise before? You don't know what you missing. Time stops here. And in the dark you can be anything you want to be. You'll see."

"Everyone wears just towels?"

"Yeah. But if I looked as good as you I wouldn't wear nothing. Just skin."

I tied the towel tight and eased off my undershorts with the towel still covering me. I kicked my shoes into the locker and locked it. Clementine moved past me, waddling up the stairs to level three where it seemed dark and quiet as I followed. The floor was cold to my bare feet. A single aisle separated rows of doors, some open, some closed. Men paraded by quietly, occasionally peeking into an open room. Clementine passed in front of me, and I peeked right and left at the tiny rooms where male bodies lay expectantly: ass or balls up. One man lay with a can of Crisco between his legs, his crooked finger inviting anyone inside. I followed Clementine. We eased along the aisle and up the narrow stairwell leading to the next level up. Level four. More rooms. This time I could hear people moan, throats gag and cough. Each room had a number like the lockers below, many more were closed, and the only sounds were those of mouths on flesh and the quiet shuffle of bare feet. Then we came upon a small hallway with even smaller lockers lining the walls. I asked Clementine about these.

"Oh, honey, you so tired. It's for memory. And masturbation. Don't you remember your first week in junior high when they assigned lockers and you fell in love with the boy who had the locker next to yours? Remember how you used to peek in to see if he had any photographs of a girlfriend, or just sniff at the opening where you thought he kept his gym shorts and jockstrap? It was your first sensual contact. Not even sexual, and you were stupid enough to call it love. We all had them in those days. Even me. Those little shit nothings who'd call us sissies and feel our asses when nobody else was looking. They didn't give a fuck about how much we ached inside, or how we pined secretly for their friendship. I'm old as sin, girl."

"Ache? I don't know what you're talking about."

"You probably don't. But desire and hurt get mixed up here sometimes. Like that guy. See how he dangles up to the cold metal? See how he rubs himself so gently, like he's touching skin?"

I watched the boy lean toward the locker, his nose at the grillwork. Forehead perspiring, beads of sweat reflecting in the dim light. Arms hugging metal.

"I don't believe you," I said.

"You don't, huh?"

"Nobody knows about Sam Levine. He used to wait for

me by the playground. We'd walk home together, so what? We'd wrestle in the park, so what? Then his Mom would call him to dinner."

"And you wanted him to hold you longer, just a minute or two longer because you were about to drip and thought it was pee, huh? Like I told you, Jesse, I'm old as sin."

"I'm going to the next floor."

The next stairwell was narrower, the air thick with steam and heat. I started to sweat. From the sound of water splashing on tile, I figured it was the shower and sauna and steam room. The real things. Naked men stood in every patch of light and sound. Soapy water ran from down their backs and into a common drain.

"This is the Saturday shower at scout camp," Clementine said in a voice more gruff than before. Another accent, maybe. "When you couldn't wait to scrub up next to the new boy on the staff. Sure, you tried back rubs and skinny-dipping in the lake at night. But that wasn't enough, was it? You wanted his whole wet body draped in light. You wanted to towel him off with your tongue. Here's your chance. Only there's twenty of them—all shapes, sizes, colors. You can take them soaped up, or wait till they're rinsed and conditioned. I like the creme rinse myself. Albert VO5."

"I've heard enough, Clem," I said, trying to look away from him and catch someone's eye. No one noticed me.

"Clementine, darling," he said in a voice like a saleslady. "Would you now like to try the quick steam or the slow cooker of the sauna? The dry heat burns just as hot. Step in. Step in. Or, you can imagine the steam is the low fog over Lake Deerfield and you rub your canoe up against any shore and hope it takes you in. Like that one, or him, or him. Reach out, honey. Touch ground. Get down and dirty like you want to be under the cover of night or fog or any other dream you have. It's all here."

And I did reach out, blindly. Out of the mist, a man appeared almost magically. Sweat from his hairy chest dripped onto mine. He bent down to kiss me. I saw that he had no teeth and that his body was folds of fat. I left the

steam room without looking back at him or waiting for
Clementine. I'd find my own fog, I thought, what the hell.
I closed the door behind me. Then I felt Clementine's hand
on my shoulder. His voice was different this time too.

"Were you looking for me?" he said. "I'm not lost. Just
overcome a bit by the heat and the heavies inside. I need air,
too. Especially at my age. You don't get much air here,
though. Let's go up another level."

We climbed further, Clementine and I. We reached the
next flight of stairs and there I saw the movement of thick,
square thighs, calves, a towel tight on a firm, mushrooming
torso. Hair wavy and brown, pale skin glistening in the half-
dark. He was climbing ahead of me. I followed.

"Metro," I said, pulling at Clementine's towel. "That
guy looks like Metro."

"Metro? This ain't no train," he said. "We going uptown
not down."

"His name was Metro."

"What kind of name is that?"

"Like Clementine," I said. "Made up."

"Like Jesse, you mean," he said, smiling a smile I didn't
want to see. His voice was different this time too. How many
more accents did he have stored away?

"I was named after my mother," I said.

"Honey, even that ain't new around here."

By this time the figure I was following disappeared behind the door to the next level. I followed. Clementine
breathed hard behind me, like he couldn't keep up. I felt his
eyes scratching the back of my neck. But when I entered the
next level, I heard voices that made me stop so short that
Clementine bumped into me, his hands bracing a fall against
my ass, the towel almost coming loose. The voices were
coming from a radio or television. It was the eleven o'clock
news televised on a six-foot screen. And sitting before it on
tiers of carpeted platforms were men lounging in all positions. The voice of the newscaster made me lose sight of the
man I was following. The newscast was loud and images
came blurred on the large screen.

When his words registered in my mind, I stood stock-still. Air became trapped in my throat, my chest and lungs. Pain went everywhere inside and wouldn't let me go. I didn't want to see or hear anything, but I couldn't help it.

"Four teenagers, suspects in the recent stabbing of a young reporter for the *Daily News,* were apprehended today in the vicinity of the murder, which occurred last week. Police discovered fifteen-year-old Lonny Russo lying naked in the chalk outline of the body this morning and brought him in for questioning. Neighbors had reported seeing him in the area several times and just hours before he was arrested. Later, police obtained a confession from him in which he named three accomplices, Max Bono, Louis Iacuzzi, and Cuddles Manzani. The others were also arrested and were arraigned earlier this evening. Bail was set at $25,000 each, but it is doubtful whether they or their families can meet it. The boys are being detained at Rikers Island until their trial date. Mr. Jon-Michael Barthé, the victim, had been with the *News* for only several months. He was an avowed homosexual, and the police suspect he may have known one of the boys. Barthé's body, following an autopsy performed at Bellevue Hospital, was flown to Louisiana at his family's request for burial there."

I saw their faces. Scary faces. Mean faces. I watched as they walked handcuffed into the police station. They didn't hide under stretched T-shirts or jackets pulled over their heads like most suspects in front of the camera. These boys walked proudly, defiantly, as if they had a world of support behind them. Metro's college graduation picture was shown, but it had been cut off at the shoulders, right where another arm could be seen draped around him, a brown hand clutching another diploma rolled with ribbon. That hand was mine. The television room was quiet, almost hushed. Some men squirmed in their seats, others were roused from their reclining positions to take notice of Metro and what had happened. I said nothing.

I turned to Clementine who was absorbed in the newscast. "It just keeps happening, huh?" he said. "Why, just last

month in Central Park some guys went around with baseball
bats and attacked people from behind. People they only suspected were faggots. Who do those fucking kids think they
are, anyway? Who are they to decide who's a faggot and
who ain't?"

"Yeah, who the hell," I said, turning from the screen
and for the first time seeing two rows of single doors. When
the news had finished some doors opened, some closed. Men
left the carpeted area for whatever retreat was available.

"Shit, baby," said Clementine. "Sometimes it's just as
bad in here as it is out there."

"What do you mean?"

"You have to find that out for yourself. Maybe for you
it won't be so bad, pretty as you are."

"Real pretty," said someone passing me. I soon lost him
to a sea of towels.

"You want to stay and see the late movie? It's *Whatever
Happened to Baby Jane?* We all say the Bette Davis lines in
unison. It's like being in church and reciting scripture."
Clementine looked delighted.

I frowned.

"Then let's go up another flight. You'll like what's there,
even if these rooms ain't much. Hold onto your fantasy. It's
gonna be a bumpy night."

"Wrong film, Clem."

"Don't I know it? I wrote the original lines, darling."

"My darling Clementine."

"Now you've got the hang of it." Clementine put his
arm around my shoulder and led me up the stairs. For no
reason at all Metro's voice came to me. The closeness was
scary.

"Hello again."

"Hello, there."

"I'm Jon-Michael."

"I remember. I'm Jesse."

I loved him. I loved his eyes. I loved his angular face and
awkward walk as if his body tilted with the weight on his

back or in his mind. His fingers were thick, nails chewed to red blunted tips, and when he brushed back his hair you could see the oval of his head smooth out from the triangular nose and square jaw. His teeth were perfect. Once he gave me a tooth. His dentist had extracted a painful wisdom tooth growing in too small a space. It was a perfect specimen, no cavities, not even a line of tartar where tooth meets gum. Metro laughed when he presented it to me. I placed it in a box where I kept my high school class ring, my frayed Boy Scout badges, my Honor Society pin. His smile, his teeth, now a jewel of his body I could keep.

Which is what I remembered most about him that cold February evening when he called out to my row of marching demonstrators as we returned to the Nkrumah Center. Later, at dinner, he came over to my table where I was sitting alone. "Did everyone make it back all right to the Center?" he asked. "No one hurt?"

"No one. Thanks for asking."

"May I join you? I'm still finishing dessert."

He brought his tray over and sat down close enough to make me nervous. I said nothing at all about the demonstration, just to be sure it was me he wanted to get to know.

"The dining hall is closing. We have a few minutes. They'll ask for our trays soon."

"You're right. They are closing."

He had an accent, somewhat disguised, but an accent just the same.

"You want to come back to my room?" I asked. "We can talk there." He seemed cautious.

"Sure. Let's go. Is it far?"

I had a single room that year. My own room, for the first time in my life. At home my brother Charlie and I shared a bedroom, and we would either be fighting or conspiring to scare my parents when we heard their regular late-night sounds from the other side of the wall. The room I now had on the second floor of Andrews Hall looked out on the campus cemetery. Abandoned, I was sure. Then one morning I saw an elderly woman place flowers at a headstone. When she left I discovered the last resting place of a retired professor of English, dead only a year. The ground beneath my feet was still soft. The headstone, unlike the moss-edged others, was so new it shimmered in the sun. I watched for her regularly from my window. She came only on Sunday mornings. She never knew I was watching, or that other rooms above mine also had eyes.

We reached my room through the tunnel connecting dorms and dining hall. I cleared a place for Jon-Michael to sit on the bed and searched for records to play.

"Jazz?"

"Sure," he said. "Classical jazz."

"Are you French? I mean, you have a French name. I'm told Europeans really have a thing for jazz."

"Can't you tell by my accent?"

"It's a mixture. Southern? British? What is it?"

"Well, I'm just a poor boy from Louisiana. Lafayette, Louisiana. Cajun Country. You know about the Cajuns of the South?"

"Nothing."

"Well, our ancestors are French. Protestant refugees from France who settled in Canada, then when the English kicked us out, many left for Louisiana which was still under Napolean's control then."

"I remember. The Louisiana Purchase. Right?"

"Right."

"How'd you manage to come to Wesman, this far east?"

"My father's a veterinarian. He wanted to go to Harvard, but his family was too poor to send him east to school. He wanted me to come east. I'm on scholarship."

"So you're one of the disadvantaged white boys of the South," I said, laughing. "Culturally, I mean. That's the way they see it, don't they?"

"Maybe. But I'm here, and glad of it."

"I'm from Connecticut. Hartford. A northern ghetto."

"Ghetto kid meets farm boy."

"Sounds like a double-feature horror flick." And we laughed. We later discovered we were both English majors.

Jon-Michael wanted to be a journalist; I, a dancer. I also majored in theater arts. But I didn't tell him then that I wanted to be a dancer. It was considered too unacademic. Frivolous. But what better way to fulfill a gym requirement without having to run track, swim, play football or soccer. And in cold New England weather! I tried tennis and barely got the ball to the other court, and I never got away fast enough from the squash ball that always found my head or foot to bang against instead of the front wall.

Then I joined the crowd of students at the "black table" for meals and had to give up telling anyone I wanted to dance. Until someone asked me why I played "B-ball" so much.

"You always in the gym, man."

"You've seen me?"

"Yeah, Jesse. You must be pretty good."

I couldn't help chuckling at the confusion. "I go to the gym for dance class."

Sudden silence.

"What?"

"Dance. I study dance."

"For what? To be a ballerina?"

The table broke up laughing. People started looking from other tables. I tried to hide. And for once I regretted there was only one black table, a gathering of friends that the *New York Times* called "Wesman's failure in liberal education," which meant that black students weren't supposed to have each other as friends. We were supposed to be "textbooks" for liberal whites, which is what my friend Randolph used to say. But who'd speak up for me? The brothers, or whites who never expected to enroll at this prestigious university near the Connecticut River with black boys from Harlem or the South as roommates? Or worse, competing for the same A in government class or freshman composition. So I was caught. And I tried to dance with words this time.

"If you knew anything about dance you'd know that ballet is only one form. One of many. You must be reading too many comic books or men's fashion magazines."

"Whoaaaah—" said someone else.

"Just vamp all over him, Jim," said another.

"My name ain't Jim," I said.

"You trying to start something, man."

"Just that it's modern dance. I study modern dance."

"Modern Dance?"

"Yeah. You know like Alvin Ailey. Merce Cunningham. Murray Louis. Pearl Primus. Modern dance."

"You still wear tights and leotards and swish don't you?"

"I thought you were smarter than that. All of you." I looked around the table.

"Dance," he said again. "Shit."

"Then you take that shit to the cleaners," I said, picking up my tray. The food half-eaten, cold. Behind me was silence, then laughter sharp as nails. But months later, when the same students organized the takeover of the classroom building and asked me to dance as part of a memorial service to Malcolm X, I refused. Yes, I was there demonstrating too, but I left the barricaded front door for the second-story window, and I looked out on my own.

When I told Clementine I had recently graduated from college he rolled his eyes in despair. He sucked his lips. "I never heard of going to no college to be a dancer. You just dance, that's all, and hope the music keeps on playing."

"Is that how you sing, to just any music?"

"I just spreads my mouth and holler. 'Specially when it goes in."

"I'm not talking about sex."

"What else is there to holler about or to spread for?"

"Metro and I were different. We met in college."

"That's what you think. You still holding on to that shit? Carrying that load? Honey, here you get your load off. Any way you can."

"Not me."

"That's cause you think you too pure to pee. But when that boy got killed you found out that he wanted to get down sometimes, huh? That he really came to the baths just to get away from you. Pretty as you is, he probably felt ugly because he knew he needed him something raw. Something you was just too refined to give up."

"That's not right, Clementine. Metro and I came from the same stuff."

"The same dirt?"

"Stuff."

"Then why are you here?"

"Because I know what Metro wanted. And I know what I want."

"That's what you think. It may be that cut-and-dry in here, but you got to bring your own lubrication."

That first evening in my room, Metro and I didn't talk long. But we discovered one main interest we had in common, literature. The next semester we found ourselves in the same English class at 8:30 A.M. and afterward arguing about poetry over coffee in the campus snack bar. Metro told me then that he had spent the summer before in France with a study group from the college. I couldn't hide the envy that came through my silence. I wanted to know everything about Paris and even dragged up remnants of my high school French to use in conversation. Metro described the city: the wide boulevards, clean subway, skeletal Eiffel Tower, and the muddy brown Seine that sometimes crests over the stretch of road circling the banks. I had always thought of the Seine as silvery and dark and smooth as wine.

Then he talked about Lafayette, Louisiana, and the farm where he grew up, and the black people who clustered in small villages nearby. Parishes, he called them. The smell of woodsmoke and tobacco hung everywhere. Blacks living there had French names, too. Then I told him about my father and grandfather, both from Pee Dee, North Carolina, where the river gave the village its name and where it runs as chalky brown as the Mississippi or even the Seine. I told him about my mother's mother who lived and died in Irmo, South Carolina, just outside of Columbia. When we went to her funeral, I was only six or seven. The only thing I remember is our changing trains in the middle of somewhere with hiss and steam rising from the tracks, and later, my mother's scratchy sobbing which was even then a language the two of us shared. "Her name is Jessica," I said. "And she named me Jesse. Boys named after their mothers are different." He smiled. And I smiled.

Late one night, he came back to my room. I had just finished typing a paper and was about to begin my dance exercises, stretching and pulling each muscle to relax for sleep. He was startled and uneasy at first to find me in tights and leotard. He watched my movements silently. He sat on the bed, his face flushed, hands nervous. I ended my last relevé repetition. I didn't say anything, either, but sat cross-legged facing him. He got off the bed and sat on the floor.

"Could you like me just a little bit?" he asked abruptly.

"I could like you a whole lot."

"I can't help that I'm from the South." He looked worried. Then he put his hand on my thigh. The warmth seeped through the stretched black cotton to my brown skin. "You look good in tights," he said.

"Let me show you how I look without them," I said.

"Do you like me a little bit?"

"I like you a whole lot."

The next morning we were late for the same class. We ran through the snow covering the ground, slipping and falling along the way. I called him Metro for the fast, slippery train we were on.

For the rest of that semester, our junior year, I took dance class three afternoons and Metro worked on the campus paper several nights a week. He wanted to become editor the following year. Sometimes we studied together all night. Sometimes we were together all night without studying.

In our senior year, Metro became editor of the paper and I performed in the college's spring dance concert. Wilona Agnes and I danced to a Billie Holiday song about a man leaving a woman and driving her to drink. And I did a solo to "Strange Fruit." I dressed in tattered cut-off jeans, baring my chest and dancing in a series of small, contracted movements in a circle that extended from a single rope ending in a noose about my neck. The spotlight held my glistening head and body. My arms and head dangled alternately from the noose. Oil on my body glistened with sweat in the light that held me as tight as the rope did against the thick suggestion of night. White makeup around my eyes made the sockets appear to bulge and my head look like a dangling skull. My movements silenced the audience, and I wasn't even sure of their presence until the last wailing chord from the song finished and my head turned in the noose and hung there limp. The house lights brightened. Applause was hesitant, then gathered weight. It was my first solo, a statement in itself of where I might go from this limited space of light and shivering movement. It was a dance I kept on dancing in my mind long after the concert. The next day someone asked me what the dance meant. I said the meaning, if there was any meaning, was obvious. Then he asked if I wasn't really saying something about people ostracized from society, outcast, martyred, some fruit unpicked and rotting in its sugar. I didn't know what to say. I promised to think it over. And I promised myself that I'd keep on dancing no matter how hesitant the applause, how rooted the tree, how strange the fruit.

Then I saw the gleam of metal prison bars on level six.

Clementine started loosening his towel, taking it off, rolling it around his neck like a scarf. He was grinning wide this time. Grinning and pulling me after him.

"You don't need a room for this action, baby. It's all out in the open."

"You mean caged in."

"That's just a figure of speech. You can do anything you want here. With one person, two, or several. I don't know about you, Jesse, but I'm getting me some action." He disappeared into the darkness. I looked around but I couldn't really contain all I saw. Instead of private rooms with numbered doors protecting the sounds and action inside, these were open spaces bordered by aluminum bars extending floor to ceiling. People lay everywhere, on bunk beds or single twin-sized mattresses covered with dark vinyl, no sheets. And every 4 × 8 space was measured out by the flat metal bars and the people in them waiting for pleasure or punishment. Men filed in and out of the cells. Some remained coupled or in threes for just as long as it took to imagine you were a prisoner and they were the guards or fellow inmates, coming to take their pleasure or revenge on your youth or safety. It didn't matter if you were lubricated or not. Or if you really wanted it that way. They took pleasure in your pain and confinement and you lay there, ass open and crying for more, more, and more.

"But you want pain," a voice inside me said. "Don't you? Why then did you come here? It's not because of Metro anymore. He's dead."

"Why did you choose that dance, Jesse?"

"Look Metro, I don't want to discuss it. It's my favorite Billie Holiday song and I wanted to dance."

"But why do you always act like black people are the only ones oppressed? There are other oppressed people."

"Like who?"

"Gays, Jews. Even poor boys from the South. Don't you think we have some weight to bear? Don't you think we hurt sometimes?"

"You're white, Metro. At a distance you blend in with the crowd. Shit, they can see me coming, and in a riot they don't stop me to ask if I've been to college or live in the suburbs. They start beating any black head they find."

"So you take it out on me."

"You've got nothing to do with it."

"Oh, yes, I do. You really think every white person is responsible. So you say no when I want to hold you. And when you make me think you're spending the night with me, you say no again so I'll feel rejection and loss. Shit, Jesse, you can't say yes, can you? Yes, you love me. Yes, we screw together. Yes, we're lovers. And yes, we're faggots. Two faggots. That's what we are."

My hands swelled into fists. My chest got so tight I could barely draw breath. I stood perfectly still.

"You want to hit me? Go on and hit me," Metro said. He stood directly in front. I could feel his breath on my skin. "Go on, hit me."

My face burned, then my eyes. I couldn't stop the tears. He lifted his arms and held me tight. Tighter than anyone had ever held me. Tighter than I knew I could ever hold myself. My chest relaxed. Air escaped my lungs in a long low sound.

"Time stops here," Clementine said, his mouth at my ear. "I'm old as sin, you know. Old as you'll be someday."

"But I won't be here."

"If you're lucky, perhaps. Most of us aren't so lucky. You'll come back like I do because this place will remind you of something or someplace or somebody."

"Metro?"

"Maybe me."

"Come on, Clementine."

"Or you'll remember yourself. Who you really are."

"I'm Jesse. I was named after Jessica."

"Tell him. The guy fondling your balls."

"I don't see him."

"You feel it, don't you?"

"The metal bars? The prison?"

"Desire rising. Your muscles going slack. Ass twitching. Balls aching to let go."

"Yes. Yes."

"You know what you are?"

"Jesse. Jesse Durand."

"What does that mean? Jesse?"

"Boys named after their mothers are different."

"Is that all?"

"No."

"What about Metro?"

"He's dead."

"And who killed him, Jesse? Who killed him inside?

Who treated him like shit until he couldn't stand his own smell?"

"Not me. It wasn't me."

"No, Jesse?"

Clementine laughed a long and deep belly laugh.

"I'm getting out of here."

"Not until you've been to Paradise."

"Where's that?"

"Up. All the way up."

I fingered my way through the darkness and followed the gleam from the metal bars to the hall light. I went up the stairs to the next level that had no number. I opened the door, and found myself in a gym with mirrors. Metal apparatus and weights and mirrors everywhere. Men in shiny gym shorts and thick socks, bulging groins, biceps, thighs, and thin waists. Barbells, universal gyms, scales, exercise mats stood ready like dance partners for aspiring musclemen. Clementine tugged at my towel. "You can tone up those muscles in here if you want. You gotta be strong for the next level. Real strong."

"I don't need it," I said. "I'm going straight up."

"Level seven? Paradise? Don't say I didn't warn you."

At first I didn't notice anything different about level seven except for the carpeted hallway and the single corridor. But there were only four doors leading to the rooms, not the usual twelve or fifteen on a floor. And why call this level Paradise? Was it more than just a name for a bathhouse? There was only one way to find out. But I couldn't decide which door to open first. I started with the closest one, just in case I needed a quick exit.

I eased the door open. Suddenly light, blinding light from what seemed like a row of high-intensity bulbs against mirrored walls. I staggered, and when I could see clearer I saw a king-size bed with disheveled white sheets and two white bodies coupling furiously. On the wall in every direction was the repeated image of the two men coupling, 360 degrees of it. Even the floor was mirrored, and the image kept repeating and repeating as if it extended into infinity. The men locked in each other's arms seemed to be enjoying immortality as much as each other. The multiplication of images and light gave me a headache. I closed the door.

The second room was decorated like an army barracks. Metal bunk beds and olive green footlockers filled the floor space. Against the far wall were rifles and military uniforms hanging by nails and hangers. From somewhere in the ceiling a Sousa march was piped in on tape with the sound of men calling out cadence. The burnt smell of ammunition was in the air. I noticed movement on the bunk beds and around the footlockers. Men dressed in uniform gahered close to me. No one spoke but I figured I could join them if I put on one of the uniforms. I remained by the door. The light from the hallway must have disturbed some because they looked at me with scorn. "Close the door, Private," someone said. "Close the fucking door."

A hand behind me closed it. When my eyes adjusted to the dim lighting inside I saw men fondling empty black boots and rifles. A man in uniform lay above another, but by the movement of their hands and mouths they appeared to be making love to the olive-drab fatigues, the steel-toed boots, the insignia rather than the men inside them. Someone started shouting commands. Another was marching in place, his eyes straight, lifeless. A voice above him: "And you, Private, what makes you think you got what it takes to be an officer?"

"Nothing, sir!"

I watched him go to his knees, his hands grabbing desperately at another man's pants, but it was the pants themselves he was after, their smell of sweat and fatigue.

"Where's you uniform, Private?"

I inched backwards toward the door. I prayed it would open.

"Where's your uniform, Private?" Then louder, "Hey, guys, he ain't got no uniform." Suddenly several pairs of eyes focused on me. I cracked open the door. A hand nearby blocked it. "Let the sergeant pass," I said in a deep voice. The darkness hid enough of my nakedness to enlarge my voice. I said again, louder, "Let the sergeant pass."

The door opened. I was in the hallway again. Safe.

The next room was a real prison cell. Beyond the open door was a grillwork of metal bars that swung freely open. Inside were more bars and a single window high above an open toilet. Graffiti in spray paint and magic markers covered the walls. The cell had a real lock and pairs of handcuffs hanging from one wall. There was a single bed and it was empty. Loose plaster dusted the floor. Several holes appeared in the wall's baseboard as if someone had tried to dig his way out or a rat was boring his way in. The room was empty, chilling in its openness. The silence took on character. I couldn't stay much longer than the few minutes it took to survey the scene. I stepped back toward the door and eased it shut. Then I heard a sound like someone crying. I looked inside again. The crying became louder, then short of breath and rapid like the breather was mounting or straining against a difficult obstacle. I could see nothing. Then the chill of silence. I closed the door and walked to the last room on the hall. The moaning continued in my mind.

The last room was decorated like a college dorm room, complete with a plaid bedspread on the single bed and football pennants tacked to the wall. Light came from a desk lamp. Textbooks lay open on the wooden desk. Next to the desk and bed was a small bookcase with notebooks and papers piled loosely on the top and bottom shelves. On the desk was an empty picture frame for stills of Mom and Dad and the family dog. I walked further into the room. The place was warm and inviting. It was as if I had actually been in that space before. I looked through the papers and books. I tested the bed, then lay down. From the hall light filling the open door, I saw a figure come toward me and stop. It was Clementine. How long he had been following me, I couldn't tell. But I felt more at ease, relaxed. He didn't enter. The light blocked a clear view of his face, but I felt him smiling, laughing.

"I see you found yours, huh, Jesse?"

"My what?"

"Fantasy Room."

"I thought this was Paradise."

"That's what they all think—"

"That paradise is fantasy, you mean, or is it the other way around?"

"Yes, until it comes true."

"Then it's no longer fantasy, right?"

"You see the real horror of it."

"How do I get out of here, Clementine?" I asked. I wasn't even alarmed. This room seemed so much safer than the others. So much like something I already knew.

"When the time comes, you'll leave."

I was already getting sleepy on the bed. "When's that?" I said drowsily.

"Good night, Jesse," he said.

"You're going?"

"You found yours. Now I'm going to get mine, like I do every Wednesday when I don't have people like you to look after. Shit, they should put me on the payroll."

"What are you talking about?"

"Never mind."

"I won't be back, you know, after this."

"That's what I said, Jesse. And that was a long time ago. Shall I close the door now?"

"Yes."

"You sure?"

"I'm all right."

The door eased shut and I lay there waiting in the half-dark. I followed the stream of light coming from the desk lamp and noticed books I hadn't seen before. One was a copy of the Norton Anthology I remembered from English literature class. I pulled it from the shelf and thumbed through the pages from the back. My eyes got heavy, tired. I replaced the book and turned down the bedspread. I lay flat and naked across the sheets. I was waiting. And I waited and waited and waited until sleep or the waiting itself would bring Metro back alive.

"Why do you call me Metro? It's not my real name."

"You were in France once."

"But why Metro?"

"Quick travel underground."

"But do you love me?"

No one thought it odd that we marched together for graduation. We were known to be good friends, both English majors. No one suspected we were anything more than that, not even when we argued about the dance and ended our fight by walking hand in hand across campus. Or when he left me in front of the all-night reserve room of the library and I walked alone back to the dorm. But before I got there I found myself leaning against the corrugated trunk of an oak tree and crying from all my weaknesses, all my fears. I didn't fear our discovery, I feared our loss and my own obstinacy about holding on to him as best I could. Maybe it was a triumph I felt later when we donned cap and gown and marched together through the Wesman gates. We were finished there, but our slow march away was also the commencement of another life, a life we hadn't dared to discuss before, until someone saw us: Vester Johnson from Mississippi, all six feet of him.

Someone crowded the light from the door left ajar. I thought it was Clementine again. "No," I said, but the figure remained in place. I saw his hand frame the door, then a head poke inside. I didn't recognize the face.

"You're late for class," he said.

"What?"

"Your eight o'clock chemistry class. You'll miss the lab instructions. You'll need a partner for the experiment."

"Huh?"

"And your library books. They're overdue. I've come to collect them."

"What are you talking about?"

"Hey, College Boy, you going to the sorority dance? Or

you want to have a mixer right here? Who won the football game? You got the score?"

"Get lost, will you?"

"Come on, College Boy, roll over. Let me give your footballs a cheer. Fe, fi, fo, fum, we're on top and number one! Catch that pass, up your ass, rah, rah, rah!"

"Get the fuck out of here!"

"Shit," he said, closing the door shut. "Now I gotta go play Army with those other guys. Or prison, and I don't want that."

Like Vester, I said to myself. Vester who saw us and wanted some for himself. He worked in the campus stationery store and changed his voice every semester to hide his Mississippi accent. He said things like "Gosh" and "Wow-ee" and pretended to be from Scarsdale where people used words like "indubitably." He used to say how he could have gone to Harvard but chose Wesman instead. Once I heard him tell someone from White Plains that he was an abandoned child and was raised by wealthy foster parents in Scarsdale. The family car this year, he said, would be a Seville. Once he saw Metro and me together, he tried to pretend he was from New York City. He asked me to his room once for smoke and drinks. While we were listening to music and getting drunk, he pressed my hand to his groin. I took it away.

"Did I do that?" he said the next day. "Really?"

"Really," I said.

"Gosh, I mean, how could I do something like that. I'm shocked!"

"I'm not," I said, standing in the doorway to his room. People from other rooms down the hall must have heard us.

"Indubitably," he said.

Two days later in the campus dining hall he told me the truth. Metro was with me but was as uncertain as I was about Vester's intentions. You could never tell what Vester was actually thinking or what he would do.

"Well, yes, I should tell you," Vester said, cutting his

roast beef into neat thin strips. "To be honest. Really," he added, stretching both vowels and consonants in another voice. He chewed a small cube slowly as if to find his words in the meat. His voice assumed an artificial dignity, a pose, munching each word. "You see, Jesse. And your friend there, too." He poured gravy over the potatoes and mixed it in.

"Me?" said Metro.

"Yes, you." Vester wouldn't call his name, or look directly at him. But his eyes tried to hold mine. I turned away.

"You see, Jesse. I never get so drunk or so high that I don't know what's happening around me." He paused, the meat tiny in his mouth. "Or what I'm doing."

Metro's back stiffened instantly. I could feel his heat and mine.

"And remember afterwards, too. Everything," Vester continued, more sure of himself with the action of the knife and teeth on meat. "I guess in the long run, I'm immune to most herb or alcohol. I've been smoking much longer than you have. You see, Jesse, people have been asking me about you. They've been curious. But not just about you. Your friend, too." He still never said Metro's name. "But I couldn't tell them because I wasn't quite sure myself. You can't be sure just because someone walks or talks a certain way. So I said I honestly didn't know. But they thought that since we lived in the same dorm last year, and for the whole year, I would most certainly know. But to be quite honest, I didn't know."

I listened without saying a word. Metro tried to eat. By Metro's slow motions I could tell that the food had suddenly lost its taste. My mouth was dry, too dry for words.

"You see, Jesse, when I want to find out something about a person, I'll do anything to find it out. I'd thought about asking you, but I knew it would be too easy for you to lie. And I simply just had to know."

My lips seemed to crack. I didn't know what Metro was thinking then, but I was scared and worried for both of us.

I looked at Vester, straight at him. His eyes pierced me like the words from his round face.

"I had to know. And when I found out what I wanted to know, Jesse," and then Vester looked sharply at Metro, then back to me, "I was *disgusted.*"

"Disgusted? But I didn't do anything," I said.

Vester rose from the table. His plate was half-empty. He kicked back the chair and stood tall. I could only stare in disbelief. I had done nothing. He walked stiffly to another table. Metro also stared after him, then at me. Metro made only the simplest gestures for control; looking at his food, fingering his throat. We said nothing. Silence was all we ate.

"Why do you call me Metro?"

"You were in France. Once."

"Why do you call me Metro?"

"You've been places where I want to go."

"Why do you call me Metro?"

"Take me, baby. Take me underground."

"Do you love me? Do you love me? Do you love me?" Another knock at the door. "Go away."

"It's me—Clementine. You all right in there?"

"Yes. I'm all right."

"I thought I heard you crying."

"It wasn't me."

"Good, because when I come back, I'm gonna be greased and ready."

"Ready for what?"

"Don't you know by now?"

I rolled on my side away from the door. The picture frames on the desk were empty, the football pennants torn. The open textbook: Jon-Michael Barthé, '75. Not Metro. But then he didn't know who I was, either. Not after commencement and his trip back home to Louisiana.

"Why this apartment, Jesse?"

"Don't you like it?"

"There's hardly any room."

"There's room enough."

"Why this neighborhood, Jesse?"

"Don't you like it?"

"Why grow your hair so long? Why the Afro pick in the bathroom? Why are all the criminals in the streets black? Why are we in New York?"

"I'm here to dance."

"I'm scared, Jesse. I'm really scared. I hate taking the subways. I hate working at night. I hate their dark faces. They're just too dark, too black."

"Like looking straight into a subway tunnel? Afraid you won't get out?"

"I'm scared, Jesse."

I held him tight in my arms that night. He was pale, thin, and more nervous than I remembered him being before. He seemed to change there in my arms into someone more fragile, more vulnerable, as if the night was wearing him down and the gray, thick asphalt was draining him daily. I kissed him. I kissed him everywhere: forehead, eyes, nose, lips, neck, nipples, navel, and there. I held him tight. His penis responded to my wet caresses, and I kissed it again and again. Metro held me, his thighs tight, his fingers knotting my hair. His moan, my moan, some kind of song from his deep chest and mine. But it wasn't a song and his chest wasn't filling with desire or love that could hold safety and assurance for us. It wasn't that, but his teeth edging like a razor on one word: "Nigger."

I froze. My stomach churned with sudden fear and heat. I reached for the light. I couldn't say anything. I looked at him. My words were slow in coming. "What did you say?"

"I said, 'nigger.'"

"You mean that, Metro?"

"You wanted it low, didn't you? You wanted it dirty. Yes, I meant it."

"But I don't understand what you mean."

"You wanted to ride the rough train, huh? Well, ride it, nigger."

"You goddamn son of a bitch."

"No, I'm Metro, remember. You call me that. You want it low. You want me to take you there. Down under. Well, down under you ain't nothing but a nigger. A coal-black nigger."

I hit him once, and I hit him again. He didn't hit me back. I hit him again, harder, so he'd hit me back, but he just lay there moaning and fighting the air. He wasn't fighting me. He wasn't even seeing me. He was pulling at himself. I stopped and watched him pulling and punching at himself and pulling and punching again until he moaned again and stopped as abruptly as he had begun. The bed was wet, his groin was wet. His hands slippery with his own semen.

"That's what you get being a snow queen." It was Clementine.

"Huh?"

"I was watching you. You must have been asleep. You were yelling 'nigger, nigger,' in some high girlish voice so I knew it really wasn't you saying that. You wouldn't call yourself a nigger, would you?"

"Who's that? How'd you get in?"

"Clementine, darling. Like I said, that's what you get being a snow queen. Don't you know white boys only want to get close enough to you so they can call you nigger to your face then have you fuck them hard up the ass to get your revenge? And you know what happens?"

"What, Clementine?"

"They put those business suits right back on, chile, and head straight back to those real estate offices or employment bureaus, and give us the same shit about not being qualified enough, or that the apartment's just been rented, or they're too tired now and if you come back to their room in about an hour they might be able to get it up for you. Shit, I know their tricks. I was one of their tricks. Now look at me."

"Metro wasn't like that."

"And no black news story ever gets decent coverage, does it? You ever read about the charitable work the Elks was doing or the Daughters of the Eastern Star? Or any black man winning a prize for something outside the stadium or the disco dance floor? Huh? We're all subway muggers and rapists and drag queens. Not men. And not black men loving other black men. Loving being black and men together."

"Not Metro. He wasn't like that."

"You was his nigger. Face it. Your college degree wasn't shit. All he wanted was your cock or your ass, but he was afraid to get it off the real streets he walked on."

"No."

"And you see this-here meat? You see it? Black, ain't it? Real black. It's greased and ready, Jesse. Fat as a Carolina sausage. Greased and ready."

"Ready for what?"

"You coming home now, baby. I'm gonna get in that ass."

"No."

"Indubitably? That's what I heard you moaning. Roll over."

"No."

"I said roll over. Spread it. People been asking me, and I got to know."

"No."

"Goddamn it. You my nigger now. I'm gonna get in that ass."

Just as he sagged onto one side of the mattress, I jumped off the other side and made it to the door, slammed it shut, and bolted down the stairs. My feet twisted against the steps, missing a few, but I kept on running, past the TV room and the sauna, past open rooms, past the exhaling mist of the steam room and its fog of memory, past everything there that descended into nothing but a row of lockers and vending machines selling Coke and cookies and condoms and KY. I got into my clothes, returned key and towel, and hit the streets. From the seventh-floor window came a voice yelling, "You mine, nigger." And there was Clementine waving a fat fist.

I walked quickly, mindlessly, until I came to the subway. The smell of burning electricity turned me right around, and I was back on the street, not knowing where I'd go next. But there was only one place I could go, the battered room Metro and I shared the last time I saw him alive. I wasn't Metro's nigger, or Clementine's. I was my own beautiful black son of a bitch.

I found West Street, dodged traffic, and entered the abandoned warehouse. And there I was, face to face with the splinters.

"Jesse. Oh, Jesse. I knew you'd come."

"Do you love me, Metro?"

"Call me baby," he said drowsily.

"Is that why you asked me here? Just to call you baby?"

It wasn't always like this, I told myself. A quick fuck in an abandoned warehouse. It wasn't always like this. Once, we strolled across campus holding hands. Once, underneath the streetlamp behind the library at the marble stairs leading onto the quad, he kissed me. Once, anyone studying all night in the reserve room or just getting high late that night could have seen us. Once, someone did. Once, we marched together in the commencement procession. Then I arrived in New York first because Metro went to Louisiana to visit his family. When he came back North he seemed different, as if the change of place had given him new eyes and a different voice. Then there was something strange and desperate about him. But I showed him, didn't I? I showed him who the real nigger was. I kept my hand closed over my palm. I wouldn't let him smell it. And I didn't have to dance that time, did I? Like I'm dancing now that he's gone. *Dancing, dancing . . .*

And he was in my arms . . . was in my arms . . .

One step, two steps, three steps together . . .

One step, two steps . . .

The footsteps were real. Shadows. Presences. Body smells. A door opened somewhere close by. I felt air all over my body, all on my skin as if someone were blowing kisses. Then, as if all the breathable air inside was sucking out, a long human gasp came from somewhere behind me. Only a choke of horror remained. "Jesse!"

I was too scared to look.

Lonny

I t wasn't just me," I told the police. Red leaves are tiny mouths falling through the sky. They dry on the ground and talk back in a scratchy, girlish voice. They say things like, "You ain't never had a chance. You ain't never had a chance." And they dirty my sneaks saying, "My boy. My boy, Christ Jesus!" Shit. You have to step on them to shut them up. You got to keep on stepping sometimes until they come off the ground and come off your shoes with a sigh. Leaves leaving. Ain't that a bitch? And then they brush back, leaving the chalk outline of a guy you want to fuck. But leaves leaving in November say, "No. No. No." And you talk back to those lips crackling underfoot, saying, "Shit man. I make my own chances. I make them myself." And they lay there scattered like blood in the street, shocked, brittle, open, and hard, like pulled teeth that won't shut up. And I get to asking myself why Moms had to be there cackling at me like that. I told her once how things happened the way they did. I told everybody and signed my name in ink where they told me to sign. Even the doctor promised me clean sneaks.

Now the leaves talk very little, or I just don't hear them as much as before. Soon they'll all go away and I can walk on lighter feet. See some sky. Never hear them voices again. Never. I'll shut them up like the guys tried to shut me up. They didn't want me to say nothing. And even Metro didn't know nothing until it was too late. I didn't realize it either until the voices came back with bodies when they locked me up to wait for trial. The bodies and the voices attacked me this time, and I had no room to hide in or get away to. No fucking where to go.

"It wasn't just me," I said when the doctor wanted me to come clean. "It wasn't just me." And I must have talked out of my head because the next thing I knew Cuddles, Max, and Lou was filing into the precinct with their sweatshirts pulled over their heads and hiding their faces from photographers. Then before the TV cameras they showed themselves off proud. Camera lights blared everywhere, and you'd think that the tiles and linoleum floors had lights on them too. Blinding lights. The officer said he was Detective Stone. I told him my name—all of it. He said it was first-degree murder and bail would be pretty high. Then they brought Moms in and she wailed up and down the halls like I was her precious somebody who ain't never been in trouble before. Which was really a lie, 'cause when the judge set the bail that high she said I'd be better off in jail anyway than home with her or out in the streets, where I'd be, mostly. The others came later and even they couldn't pay bail. Not Cuddles, Max, or Lou. But they never signed their names like I did, which started all this shit. Which had started for me when the leaves was talking, and what was I gonna do but talk back. Tell them everything. The others said they wasn't guilty. That I'd done it by myself. But when some doctor said there was too many stab wounds on Metro to come from one person and that even though he was drugged up with Valium and Librium and shit to calm him down, he died of the stab wounds from different knives. You know, knives of different lengths. Not the clean knife I dropped running out of there. So it wasn't just me, I said. In fact, I don't remember it being me at all.

It was just a blowjob. Just a crazy running in the streets. My knife was clean. They must know that. It was clean. My fingerprints, if there was any, was on his head, holding it, and in his thick hair when it got to feeling good and I couldn't stop myself. Then his voice made the air thick. He was screaming. But I couldn't breathe and I couldn't stop hearing him crying or touching the red coming out of him bent up with Max and Lou at his back. Then I was alone with him. Metro. I found my feet and used them. Shit. I made room for myself. I got the hell out of there.

But it didn't end with running or dropping the goddamn knife that was clean. I went back to him. Maybe just to touch him, but he wasn't there. Only a chalk outline of his body bent like a leaf. Round and scraggly. The police found me and brought me here to face the others. And when we was left alone, like there was a goddamn signal I didn't read, they was all on me, doing an Irish jig on my head. Shit. Just 'cause I signed for myself and told what had happened. Just 'cause my knife dropped clean to the ground, just 'cause I heard them leaves falling and they sounded like lips calling my name, saying, "Lonny, Lonny," and saying, "I never touched you, man. Never." And when I told the doctor about it, he said they'd stop talking like that. And them leaves did stop talking like that for the split second before Maxie's fist found my jaw and Cuddles squeezed at my throat. Moms in night court was squeezing, too. And Moms in the visitors' gallery was yelling all out of her head and mine in the same scratchy voice, "He ain't never had a chance, Christ Jesus." Which was a lie. I had my chance. Better than that, I took my chance, Moms, and I'm gonna tell everybody about it. You all hear me out there? "Shit. I took my chance. I'm self-employed."

The one who ain't had a chance wasn't me at all. It was Metro. That's something I knew about all along. Which probably explains how I got to jail in the first place and why I even went back where they stabbed him. I wanted to tell him he never had a chance. I did, and I took my chance. And if Cuddles didn't have his knife on me, or if Maxie and Lou was really friends like I thought they was and not the crumbs they turned out to be, I'd have stopped them then and let Metro go. We was just gonna fuck him up a little bit, you know? But I didn't stop them. I couldn't. Don't ask me no more how it happened. Don't ask me no more about who he was to me, 'cause all I know is what he was and what I hate. Telling me his real name didn't change nothing. Not like he wanted things to change. Get to know me maybe. Talk shit and get high. Chase cock, not pussy. So why was I even watching Cuddles fuck that whore up near Columbus or hiding my face in his denim jacket? I was really hiding in it, you see. Cuddles ain't nothing to me. He proved that when he made his steel talk in my face. Not stainless this time cause it could have been my blood on the blade. Or my ass open like that for all the craziness Maxie and Lou had stored up inside them. It could have been me. Which is what I told myself when I was alone in the cell and nobody was looking and I could rub smooth the bruises Cuddles left on me. Not just the prick of steel. They didn't allow that in there. But the hammer of his hands and backhand jabs hard to my stomach and head. And the guards? Shit. They just pretended I wasn't even there. Your ass ain't worth shit around there. 'Specially if people are holding crap against you. And when you find out the hard way that your friends ain't your friends, you take your own chances cause you're the only one you rely on from then on. You go solo.

"Only thing worse than a faggot is a stool," Cuddles says.

"A stool faggot," goes Maxie.

"So you told them, huh? You probably told them about the herb, too. You must have told them everything," says Lou.

"I signed, goddammit! I signed my fucking name. Yeah, I told them. You guys never saw that guy Metro. You never looked back. You never heard the sound of leaves falling red or curling up dry on the goddamn ground. Don't give me none of that stale shit."

"You yellow, Lonny."

"But who was fucking him, Max? Who was fucking him?"

"Shit."

"Yeah, a great, big, stool faggot."

"If I'm a stool then what are you? All of you?"

But they wouldn't let up. They got in close. I called the guard over and he acted like he didn't hear me. He didn't move from the door. The rooms was close and hot and they was crowding in on me. The guard watching away from us, watching the outside. Cuddles's fist came first. I swung back. Caught Lou and swung again. But Maxie had me then. He had me from behind. Fists dancing on me. I couldn't feel my teeth anymore.

"You ain't gonna fuck with me!" I yelled.

The guard finally came over. "Cut that shit out," he said. "Cut it out."

But Maxie held tighter. The guard looked away. I couldn't move my hands. Cuddles and Lou at my face again until my eyes closed on red and my throat got tight with spit and acid coming up from my belly. I tasted blood. I ate it. And it was mine. Mine.

I couldn't open my eyes for two days. I could hardly eat. They had me go to the infirmary for a few hours. Then sent me back the day I had a visitor. Someone I wasn't planning on seeing ever again. Moms. She was there with my sister Patty. I didn't want to see them. Not the way I was looking. I could barely walk to my place behind the glass booth when, suddenly, she saw me and wouldn't keep her mouth shut from screaming. Her screams were metal, metal on metal, knives on knives. I held my head. I couldn't say nothing 'cause my mouth was still purple and fat and would let only air come through, and even that hurt. But she kept yelling at me, making my head hurt worse. "Look, Moms," I said to myself and to her silently through a swollen mouth, hoping she could hear me somehow, even if the words never came. *"I'm doing it. I'm taking my chance."*

"My boy! Christ Jesus. Look what they done to my boy."

My knife was clean. I never stabbed Metro. I was caught in it as much as he was. I never stabbed him, really. Really. But that's what Maxie is saying, and Lou and Cuddles too. Maybe they'll believe me 'cause I'm youngest. The public defender didn't listen to me. "They got your confession," he said. "You might as well come clean." Come clean, come clean. Shit. Everybody wants you to come clean like you nothing but shit anyway. My knife dropped on the ground. I went back to see him. I went back to touch him, like he wanted to be touched. I was there, wasn't I? Inside his shape? I was inside the print of his hands and feet and head. I was lying inside all of him. And the cold in that chalk shape was mine.

After they beat me I got put in a separate cell. The cops told me that I was going to a juvenile home upstate until the trial date. I don't know what's going to happen to the others. I don't give a fuck. Cuddles wanted it big. Let him have it big. I only signed because they said it would be easier if I went along with the cops and told what happened, told what I did and what they did, which is all I said. What I didn't expect was to see it all typed out on a page all neat and clean like a government paper for somebody's file. Mine. And I didn't expect to be locked up this long either, just 'cause we couldn't pay bail. The doctor who talked to me said they'd transfer me upstate, but there wasn't no room there just yet, no openings. I'd have to stay put for a little longer until something could be done. Something arranged. We're in separate cells. I don't know nothing about the others. We met together only once after they beat me. The guard was watching them differently that time.

What did I expect out of those bums, anyway? What did I expect out of the cops and guards? Wasn't I looking on when they stabbed Metro? Didn't I know it was going to end up like it did? How the hell could I blame anyone? I had red on myself now. Red eyes. Swollen red lips. A head that wouldn't stop pounding at the slightest footsteps. And all you could hear is feet dragging on metal. My feet dragged too. But inside the metal catwalk the floor is concrete. Walls are cinder blocks stacked high and glazed with gray paint. Each one measures twelve inches by six inches. And there are thirty blocks on the wall below the metal bars and window. One window. I've seen some cells that are just metal and air. Then some with walled metal slats for ventilation.

Space for names and fingers, maybe. Nothing else. And one square lock to remind you how far the space goes out, how far you can walk forward without coming back, then walk back again. One five-step run from locked bars to back window. Then an iron-pole bed, an open toilet, and me. Five steps this way, five steps that way. *Step-touch, step-touch, step-touch back.* And the pacing, the pacing back and forth, back and forth inside my head.

Dancing

PART THREE

Ruella

I got to the Village on the #1 train, all out of breath and with sweat in my hair. I found Jesse in a dirty warehouse room at the top of two flights of broken stairs. The place was scary. Truth is, I never would have gone to a place like that, day or night. Not me. And not without someone like Jesse on my mind. What would I look like wandering around abandoned piers and overturned garbage cans? As it was, I still didn't want to enter the building once I found it. And even after making up my mind to do so I stopped first in what looked like a hall and called his name. "Jesse?" Next up another flight of stairs. "Jesse?" Then I found a cracked open door and peeked inside. "Jesse!" The air went straight out of my lungs. He like to throw me for a loop.

He was lying on the floor in dance tights. His chest was bare. His street clothes were tossed in a pile. Broken floorboards and splinters were everywhere. "Jesse, are you all right?" He said nothing and looked at me like I wasn't even there. "It's me. Rooms. I mean, Ruella."

Slowly his eyes began to focus. He murmured something I didn't get. "I had to get away," he said.

"But why this place? I've never seen any place like it. Not from the inside, anyway."

"Metro brought me here once. He asked me to meet him and I was here with him the day he was killed. We danced."

"Well, I'm taking you home. Now get dressed. You'll catch cold."

"I was dancing. Right here. For a little bit, anyway."

"Look, Jesse. We've got an audition to make. Remember?"

I looked at his feet. They were cut and bleeding. I couldn't look long without feeling I'd be sick right there. There were splinters all on his legs and tights. He shrugged his shoulders.

I tried to coax him into his clothes and out of that awful room where drafts and sagging floorboards boxed him in. He didn't want to leave at first, as if someone was holding him there. I knew it was Metro, or the memory of him. But what dance could they possibly have done together that last afternoon, the day before Jesse called me frantically and I said, "Come on over, chile, I got plenty of room"? I can see now why he needed so much space. Much more than I could ever give.

"What about Metro?"

"Metro's dead, Jesse. And they've caught the killers. Detective Stone called yesterday. He wants to see us. And there's the audition, Jesse. God, let's get you out of here."

"I was his nigger."

"What?"

"He called me a nigger, Ruella. Then he came here looking for other niggers. White niggers and black niggers. Anyone more street than I was. That's what he needed. I was something he couldn't stand in me or in himself anymore."

"I don't know what you're talking about."

"Shit. At least I do for once. What a goddamn fool I was."

"You loved him?"

"Yes, I loved him."

"That makes all the difference," I said. I gathered up his things and pushed him out in the air. "Now, come on, Jesse. Let's go home."

We took a taxi uptown to my place. I made Jesse take a shower and sleep. I did my exercises alone again. The next morning we were back at the precinct. Detective Stone greeted us eagerly, as if arresting those guys was the easiest thing they had to do, showing how prompt and professional the officers were. I didn't like his smile. It hesitated at the corners of his mouth then wrinkled out.

"Well, we got them. All of them," he said proudly. He showed us mug shots of four boys who couldn't have been more than sixteen years old. Truth is, only two were that young. The others looked older than Jesse or me.

"We found the first guy crazy out of his head. He's the one who confessed."

"And the others?" Jesse asked.

"They came later. You've seen these guys before? Somewhere in the neighborhood?"

"Yes. They stopped me once. It wasn't a mugging or anything like that, just name-calling. Harassment. If you could have someone arrested for calling you a nigger or a faggot, the jails would be too full. I should have tried to fight back. But it was four of them, maybe five. I was new to the neighborhood. This guy wasn't one of them though." Jesse pointed to the guy who appeared the youngest.

"You're probably right," said the detective. "He's the strangest one. We found him lying naked in the chalk outline of the body. He must have been waiting for us before the neighbors called the police. He acted like he wanted us to take him away and make everything all right."

"Will I have to testify?" asked Jesse.

"You may have to answer a few questions about your friend. But you won't be actually testifying against them. They'll contact you about the trial date. I don't know when it is."

Just then I felt funny, like what could I do? "Are they out on bail?" I asked. "I wouldn't want to run into any of them." I looked at Jesse, but he was studying the photographs again and watching the detective.

"You have nothing to worry about, Miss," said the detective.

"Thank you, Detective Stone," said Jesse.

Then I said thank you and followed Jesse out of the office and the precinct building without saying anything more. It was chilly outside and the trees had few leaves. We walked to the subway. Jesse seemed relieved, his feet light. This time he actually smiled. "Let's get a warm drink," he said. "We deserve one."

We went to the Peacock Café. I took a window seat and pretended we were in Europe somewhere. I had a large cappuccino. Jesse had Mexican hot chocolate with whipped cream. With his waistline, he could afford it. Not me.

"The saddest thing," I said, "is that those guys are so young. They're kids, really. What do they know?"

"They know enough to kill," Jesse said. "When killing is a cure. Especially for something you just can't live with."

"A cure?"

"For what they may feel inside them. Confused about who they are, so they end up doing anything just to find out what it takes to be a man."

"And when they see someone who's different—"

"They attack. They've caught something inside them. Who, at fifteen, wants to be called a faggot?"

"Really," I said, rolling my eyes. "I hope they stay locked up for a long time." But then I remembered Phillip and tried to take back what I said. Change it at least. "Well, until they learn different."

Jesse finished his drink before mine was even half-empty. He looked lost in thought. Then he asked if I'd like to see the apartment. His and Metro's. I wasn't sure he'd ever want to return there. But he had left a few things behind. "I have to send some of Metro's stuff to his family. I have to do it sometime. I think I can return there now."

"You sure it's gonna be all right?"

"Let's go," he said. His calm seemed difficult to believe.

It was hard to imagine Metro's murder in that neighborhood. But in New York City things can happen anywhere. In New Jersey, too. Truth is, we were all living dangerously. Just look at Phillip, my own brother. I mean, he'd probably push drugs in our neighborhood, right where we grew up, if he had a chance. He didn't have to go all the way to Manhattan. But I didn't tell Jesse that, not yet anyway. I just studied his apartment and the sunlight from the

Rooms

windows. His three rooms at the back of the building made the entire place as bright and as quiet as a greenhouse in Connecticut. There were many plants but some were dead from lack of care. If I lived there, I'd never leave.

"Metro was the plant man, not me."

"You could have brought them to my place," I said. "Maybe we can still save a few. Some have a little green left." I took cuttings from a spider plant and a hardier Swedish ivy. I looked from the living room windows at the backs of other buildings. One window had a gate pulled shut from the inside and protected the place from the fire escape. But I didn't think of protection, really, in that sunny, open space. I thought of Phillip again, looking from his cell. I thought of Jesse. The rooms were suddenly quiet. "Jesse?"

I walked into the back bedroom where there was only a bed and a small writing table. I found him staring into a full closet. Some were Metro's clothes, some his; I couldn't tell. By the way Jesse stared at them with something like confusion, I wasn't sure even he knew which clothes belonged to whom. His eyes were red, heavy. "You all right?" I asked.

"It's not over, is it?" he said.

I didn't know what to say. I thought about Phillip. "You'll always miss him, like I missed someone once," I said.

"Someone you loved. But someone you also hated at the same time?"

"Yes, Jesse. Love and hate."

"I'm glad you're here, Rooms. I couldn't have come here alone."

"I'll help you. Gather Metro's things, I mean."

"Tell me about him."

"It's Phillip, my brother. I wanted to forget him and I couldn't. Even when I hated him the most I couldn't stop loving him."

"What happened?"

"We danced."

"You and Phillip?"

"You and me, Jesse," I said almost holding my breath.

Then he looked at me and smiled. His eyes were clearer now. His arm found my waist and he squeezed tight. I held his head and we stayed like that for a moment without saying anything more.

"I'm glad we danced," he said.

"I want you to meet Phillip."

"Why?"

"Just to know him, and know a little more about me, that's all. He's part of me like Metro's a part of you."

"He would have liked you very much, Rooms. Just like I do."

We packed as much as we could in suitcases and cardboard boxes. Jesse labeled them and telephoned the Greyhound Package Express to deliver them South. He'd send them C.O.D. But he kept the photographs, the letters, books, and typewriter. Why? He wouldn't say. We went back to my apartment for the night. We exercised. We slept.

It wasn't easy getting Jesse to visit the prison with me. Truth is, I didn't know when I'd be going myself until just before class one afternoon a letter came from Rikers saying Phillip had been transferred there. He's now in a prerelease program and getting counseling to adjust to the outside before he actually goes before the parole board. I had to look on a map to find out just where Rikers was. It's an island, like Manhattan. But there was no rapid transit to get there, no subway. We'd have to take a bus. I didn't want to go alone.

Little by little, I told Jesse more about Phillip. Little by little, I learned something more about Metro. Yet in the silent stretches between our tights and leg warmers, exercising on the floor, I felt something was missing between us. It was missing from our dance and what we talked about.

"I've told you about Phillip," I said as we left the apartment for class. It was the last regular class before company auditions.

"I've told you about Metro."

"But not everything. You haven't said anything about what happened the last time you saw him."

Jesse said nothing. He searched his bag again for the tights he told me he'd forgotten. He searched for the key to his studio locker. But just as I figured, he had everything in place.

"It's not enough, you know, being silent," I said. "And it's not enough to look out of windows. You got to be in the air, Jesse. Dance on it, even."

"I was in the air. With Metro. Only he never again touched ground."

"Maybe you were his ground. Maybe you moved out of the way or couldn't hold him anymore. Silence can do that."

"Maybe he wanted to crash."

"I don't think so. It could have happened to Phillip, too. It almost did. I was silent with him for too long. That's why I went to see him upstate. We had to touch ground with each other. I needed it more than him."

Then I told Jesse about the time Mama beat Phillip and how I did stuff for him when he first started to steal. Not that I stole, too—I just didn't say anything and let him know it was all right. Mama used to take both of us shopping, and Phillip always ended up home with something extra in his pockets. And when he'd find money in anybody's room he'd claim finders-keepers. Most of the time I'd watch in wonder at how he got away with it, even in his own mind. I guess I was saying it was fine as long as he got away with it. But one day in the grocery store, Mama found out.

We were just about to leave the check-out counter when a white salesman stopped Phillip and asked for the candy bars he'd seen him take.

"What's in your pockets, young man?"

"Nothin'."

"I saw you take those Hershey bars."

"Naw, I didn't."

Then Mama jumped into the scene and cussed the man out, saying don't be calling her boy no liar and no thief. But when we got in the car Mama saw from the rearview mirror that Phillip was eating Hersheys, and she knew she didn't buy any. She turned the car around in the middle of the

street and headed right back to the supermarket. She dragged
Phillip out of the back seat and hauled him inside. I could
see Mama and Phillip through the huge plate-glass windows. Phillip was saying something to the clerk with his
head bowed down and sniffling through his nose. I could
tell he was crying or pretending to cry. Mama was making him say aloud, "I am a thief, I am a liar." Then Mama
slapped him good right there, which made him holler for
real. She paid the man for the candy and hurried Phillip
out of the store. I kept watching the white cashier watch
Mama and Phillip leave. He shook his head with pity, then
he chuckled back to his post. Just then I swear I saw him
slip the extra dollar in his pocket before he rang up the next
sale.

Mama sped us home, more out of her embarrassment
than real need. As soon as we got there, Phillip jumped out
of the car and tried to run away. Mama caught up with him
and started beating him right there in the driveway. He broke
away from her. She ran after him, chasing him around the
house and beating him again. Her hand hurt, so she found a
fat stick and swung it against his arm. I ran after them but
stopped as soon as I heard the stick crack against him, and
both Phillip and Mama cry out like somebody was shot.
That's when I saw Phillip dance and Mama dance. I saw how
easily somebody could get electrocuted with pain or anger
and step all out of himself. Mama ran into the house. I ran
to Phillip. I held him tight in my arms, but he kept dancing
against me like he was having a fit. I hid Phillip in my room
until Mama calmed down. We heard her crying from the
kitchen and praying out loud, "Lord, don't make me that
mad again. Please Lord, don't ever make me hurt my boy
again. Don't make me hurt him."

Years later Mama had stopped praying, but she never
struck Phillip again. Phillip went right on stealing and hustling, then later dealing drugs as far as California and back,
until he was arrested in Manhattan and sent away. I told
Jesse, "Phillip isn't dancing any more."

After class we learned the date and time of the audition,

and Jesse said he'd come with me to Rikers. The bus we took was crowded.

Phillip was glad to see me this time. He even waved before he reached our visiting booth and parted with a buddy who must have had friends at another table. The other prisoners and families were black mostly, and some were really very young. A certain looseness about the visiting procedures certainly was different from Comstock. But what did I know? I was only a visitor. I'd never seen the inside. Phillip was in a good mood and he seemed glad to see me with Jesse, who was silent most of the trip out. I introduced them.

"So you're the lady's man," Phillip said. I was glad he didn't say "Lil' Sis." They shook hands. I grinned. "You looking out for my Lil' Sis?"

Then I blushed, wiping my hand across my face.

"She's looking out for me," Jesse said.

"You a dancer too, huh?"

"Yes."

"You must be pretty good. Ruella's told me and she's real proud. Proud of herself too. Just like me. I tell everyone here I got a sister who's a dancer."

"We have to audition for the company first," I said, holding onto Jesse's arm for luck. "The season starts this spring when they premiere new works."

"Maybe I'll get to choreograph something, who knows?" said Jesse.

"First we have to make the company," I said.

"You'll make it, Lil' Sis." Then Phillip turned to Jesse. "I heard about your friend. I'm sorry about that. People get mugged in the city all the time. You're not from New York, are you?"

"Mugged?" Jesse said. He looked at me with a hint of anger.

"Yes," I said quickly. "I told Phillip that Metro was mugged."

"Oh," said Jesse in a lower voice. "I see."

I held Jesse's hand again, but he slipped it away and into

his pocket. He wouldn't look at me but turned again to Phillip with a more serious look. "Yeah," he said. "They caught the kids who did it. Somebody confessed. Then they couldn't put up bail."

Phillip seemed agitated then. "Somebody always confesses," he said. "They make a deal. Everybody makes a deal."

"You'll be out soon?" said Jesse.

"I'm in prerelease now. That's a counseling program. It's supposed to get us psyched up for the outside."

"You'll be out soon," I said. And I pressed my hand firmly to the Plexiglas separating us.

"In about two months. That's when I come up for parole. Then it's off to a halfway house somewhere in the city. I'm finishing my training for auto mechanics. They like for you to have a job all set up when you leave."

"You have good family waiting for you. You have Rooms. You'll be all right."

"Rooms? I don't need no boardinghouse," Phillip said. He started looking past Jesse and me like he was trying to see the outside. Beyond the visitors' door, that is.

"I mean Rooms," Jesse said, pointing to me. "She'll take good care of you."

"That's what he calls you?" Phillip asked. He looked disturbed.

My silence answered for me.

"I don't like that. You're not a place. Shit, you're a person."

"It's just a nickname between us," Jesse said. He took my hand this time and held tight. "I started it."

"I still don't like it. I mean, I been watching these cinderblock walls and electronic gates for too long now. You get tired of a place real quick, man. Quicker than you get tired of a person."

"Jesse and I have an understanding," I said.

"Shit," Phillip said. "It's my fault, isn't it?"

"What fault, Phillip? I'm grown now. I know what I want."

"Like I did, huh? And look where I'm at. No California sun, just New York City roaches."

"It could have been different," I said.

"Shit. I wanted something special for you, Ruella. Being your brother was the hardest damn thing I had to be. I wanted you to know you was special, pretty, for me and maybe somebody else. Somebody who'd appreciate you."

"Like Jesse?"

"Can he make you happy?" He turned to Jesse. "Can you make her happy, Jesse? I'm asking because I really fucked up at it."

"Not when you ask me like that, Phillip," Jesse said. "I can't even make myself happy most of the time."

"We try, that's all we can do," I said. "But I know how to make myself a little happier. Dancing. You wait till you see me dance, Phillip."

"I hope I can," he said. His eyes scanned the visitors' room again and settled at the far end where a friend of his sat with family. I watched, too. "If I get out," he said, talking more to the air around us than to Jesse and me.

"You mean, *when* you get out, right?" said Jesse.

Phillip smiled. He started to laugh. Then his eyes dimmed as if he suddenly realized something. "It's still pretty tough. Things change here every day. You get used to monotony, routine, and you're tricked into thinking nothing's happening. But that's when you'd better watch out. Guys get stabbed here, beat up. Get their asses kicked just for the hell of it. And right when their bid's about done."

"Bid?" I asked.

"Time," he said. "Time on the inside."

"You'll be out soon," I said, smiling. "Just in time to see me dance. Jesse, too. Isn't that right?"

"Right," said Jesse.

"Then I got something to hope for."

"You'll stay with me," I said. "There's plenty of room."

Then Jesse looked at me funny, like he knew something I didn't. "You're family," I said to Phillip.

"My Lil' Sis. She won't let her brother down this time."

"Call me Lady. I like that better."

We were about to leave then, but another prisoner entered the visitors' section and patted Phillip on the back. He looked at me and held my attention for a moment. He was gorgeous. Full mustache and beard, eyes like seashells. Phillip's voice startled me. "Ruella, this is Abdul, my running buddy. My partner."

Then I remembered where I'd seen him before. Comstock. The last time I saw Phillip. Wasn't he the one who led Phillip back into the cell block after my last visit? Calmed him down just by being with him when I wasn't. When I too had forgotten how far away time and family are when you're locked up. Truth is, I didn't know how Phillip felt about me then. I smiled back at Abdul. "Isn't that a Muslim name?"

"Yeah," he said. "Around here you gotta be something or you lost, man. Real lost."

I smiled again. "I'm glad you and Phillip aren't lost."

He smiled and turned to Phillip. "So beauty runs in the family, huh, my man?"

"Oh, I'm not pretty," I said, too quickly, I think.

"You're not the best judge," said Abdul. "Ain't that right?" he asked Jesse. And Jesse said yes, but he was so distracted by other prisoners coming in that he didn't seem to notice what was happening between us. I was glad he didn't.

"You was too young to remember Daddy," Phillip said. "He was the handsomest one."

"Then I can't be that bad," I said, laughing. And Abdul laughed also, showing all his teeth and watching my mouth get bigger in a grin. But I stopped laughing when a young boy entered the room. His eye was bruised badly and one side of his face was purple. Someone shrieked from the other end of the visitors' gallery.

"My boy! Christ Jesus, what have they done to my boy?"

And her shrieks got louder as the boy walked toward the woman leaning frantically out of a younger girl's arms. The boy's mouth was so swollen he could hardly speak.

"My boy! Christ Jesus! What have they done to my boy? Lonny? You all right? Christ Jesus." And she sobbed louder, the tears choking her voice. I couldn't stop watching them, and neither could Phillip and Abdul. Then Jesse said, "It's him."

I froze.

"It's him," Jesse said again. "I'm sure of it. He was one of them." His words caught in the air.

"God, no," I said. But watching the boy fidget his way to a seat and sit cautiously as if he hurt all over, I tried to imagine the face and disheveled hair from the police mug shot I'd seen. Then I knew him. Lonny. The one who had confessed. Phillip and Abdul both stared at Jesse and me staring at him. Lonny didn't seem to know what was going on.

"He ain't never had a chance. Christ Jesus! My Lonny ain't never had a chance." The girl held the woman in closer, but she kept sobbing and crying as if she were the only mother in the room. Lonny didn't say anything. He just sat there with his head in his hands as if he couldn't even remember why he was there. "My Lonny ain't never had no chance." They said nothing together. The mother continued sobbing, and Lonny, like a battered machine, got up from the table and started out.

Just then Jesse shot up. "And what about us?" he yelled. He was out of the booth and yelling at the top of his voice. "What the fuck about us? What about me, goddamn it?"

I tried to make him sit down and shut up. He pushed me away.

"You know me? Your friends know me? Murderer! Why did you have to kill him? Why? You greasy little punk, you shit-faced motherfucker!" And Jesse was lunging at him like a lizard after a roach, trying to climb the glass wall of the booth. A guard came from behind. Phillip saw him first.

"Cool it, man." Phillip said. "Cool it."

"You'll get us screwed too," said Abdul.

But it was too late. The guard was on Jesse and hustling him out of the door. Jesse kept lunging back before the door closed. Then it did, with the clang of a lock.

"You better go, Lady," Phillip said. But before I could

get my things together another guard was upon me. "And you, Miss?"

"I'm visiting my brother here. I'll only be a minute more."

"Visitors who can't behave don't come back," he said in a gruff voice.

"I'm sorry, sir. I won't be long." He left and I settled back down. I thought of Jesse waiting outside. I hoped he was waiting outside and not locked up somewhere for disorderly conduct. "Can they lock you up for that?" I wondered aloud.

"No," said Phillip. "But what's eating your friend?"

Then I told them the whole story. As much as I knew, anyway. I told them why Jesse said that boys named after their mothers are different, how I met Jesse and he started calling me Rooms, how Metro was Jesse's lover, how Lonny and the others stabbed Metro late one night. Phillip said nothing at first. And when I finished talking I was sure he'd hate Jesse for being gay, or me for being a part of the mess. But he didn't say that. He just looked at me, then looked at Abdul for a long moment.

"You know, Lady, a man sometimes will do anything for love. A woman too, I guess. And who's to say who you can love and who you can't." Then Phillip looked straight into my eyes, and I tried to say with my eyes that I loved him, and that I loved Jesse too for what he was. "Sometimes a man just wants to lie there and be loved, Lady. And it don't much matter if it's a man or a woman doing the loving."

"And that boy," said Abdul. "Lonny. He killed Metro?"

"Yes. Well, he confessed. He was part of a gang," I said.

"And they were all arrested?"

"Shit," said Phillip. "No wonder they kicked his ass, or had somebody else in here kick his ass. They always get them after a while. Vengeance is a bitch in here. It's part of the danger. And people don't forget. It's like time done stopped. And people take grudges out on you when you least expect it. You don't have no privacy here. You got open toilets, open cells you can look through to an open bed, the roaches, and open showers. You ain't ever alone. Not even taking a shit."

"Right," said Abdul. "Here you got to be something. Anything. Just to protect yourself. Just so you know who you are."

"Or you lost, man. Real lost," said Phillip.

Suddenly, I was scared for Jesse. I really hoped he was waiting outside. "I better see about Jesse," I said, getting my things together. "Here are some cigarettes. Give some to Abdul, too."

"See you again, Lil' Sis? I mean, Lady."

I smiled and Phillip smiled back. "I'll try. I'll really try." Phillip and Abdul got up to return inside, and I watched them walk more closely together than I remember seeing before. I left the visitors' gallery, and I could still hear the old woman sobbing more quietly now from the far corner. The young girl was stroking her bent head. "He ain't never had a chance," she kept saying, more to herself now.

I found Jesse waiting outside. His eyes were dry, stony, his hands calm at his side.

"I'm going back to West 4th Street," Jesse said.

"Want me to come?"

"No."

"Jesse, don't be angry with me. I didn't know Lonny would be there. I just wanted you to meet Phillip."

"I need to be alone now."

"Call me later?"

"Yes. I'll call you later."

"You're not holding something against me, are you?"

"No."

"Men always hold things in. Or they share it only with other men."

"What?"

"Pain."

"Well, it hurts, Ruella. It really hurts."

Truth is, it hurt me too. I thought Jesse knew that. I

thought he was different from the others, those men who make a secret border of their pain, as if you could actually touch it and make it worse. But what about a man's borders when another man touches them? Maybe it's just to keep women out. Protection, maybe. No woman intrudes that far, and even if another man does, he can still heal himself in that secret sharing. Some heal themselves by wearing track shoes and jogging outfits or playing basketball on Saturday afternoons. Others by wearing leather or cowboy outfits or denim with full key rings hanging from their belts. Women carry their wounds with less fear. We bear children. That's how we stay alive. But being alive hurts. And with that pain you got to just keep on dancing, even if you dancing solo.

Dancing solo requires your own motion. You follow your own lead. Isn't that what Phillip was saying? Isn't that why Jesse wanted to shuffle-step all over Lonny's face? Others had got there first, the heel-step, heel-step, toe-step down. And what about me? Lil' Sis, Rooms, a place they all came to in their pain? What about Lady? And Missy? Where was I leading myself? I hate walls. I hate ceilings and heavy window moldings. I hate panes of glass all covered with metal gates to keep the burglars out and hold you hostage inside. I want to be in the air. Make a space out of movement. A space I can even break if I want. But give me one good arabesque or five o'clock extension—which is only frozen flight, isn't it?—or one honest leap into a man's waiting arms, and I find out too late that the ground is clay or the man is not strong or willing enough to take my weight.

I took the subway. I descended underground. Occasional flashes of light from local stations. Darkness everywhere on the express. Motion. Screeching movement. Bodies frozen on seats or with arms tangled in the metal grips for anchor, for something to hold on to, for anything, really, to stop the steady rush of darkness and fear. I had come out of the subway then with the address of the pier on a tongue of envelope. I had climbed the broken stairs. I had found Jesse and brought him back. But he didn't come back to me. And I didn't come back to Phillip, like I promised.

Jesse stayed in my rooms until the space was nothing but pain. The pain of his remembering the dance that killed Metro and sent him to me. And what am I left with? Two rooms that feel empty. A drug criminal for a brother. A handsome man needing refuge. I thought I could get higher than that if I danced well. What magical space can music and quick feet or stretched muscles of leg and torso create now? I took the leap anyway. I dragged Jesse with me to Rikers Island. But neither Jesse nor Phillip knew I was heading their way, that my one long leap before the final curtain was a lunge-*two-three* into their waiting arms. But their arms were weak, their thighs bent in grand plié. And I fell right to the ground.

Lonny

I used to think that all you had to have was your own space. Then everything would be all right. Once you had your space you could build things, like my old man did. But he found out he knew more about other people's spaces than he did his own. Before he realized it, the place where we lived got too crowded. Then he died. He didn't have a chance to do anything. But why talk about Pops. All he knew was work anyway. And there he was building spaces for everybody else instead of taking care of his own. He had a chance, yeah. Got lost in it. He found out too late that he couldn't even get invited back to the houses he painted or the garages he built on slabs of concrete no bigger than this one but without the bars. Pops built things—he brought space to life. I guess the walls just closed in on him at home, and being poor must have kept him away from the inside of anywhere else.

Now, I was on the inside. On a chance I took myself. Moms couldn't make bail. Nobody could. So we had to lay there until the trial. Until I could get away upstate. I could have told Moms just how I felt and told her not to worry since she said herself that I'd be better off inside these walls than out on the streets—away from the freezing meat-packing warehouses and the slimy platforms where they load the meat onto trucks or take meat off the truck and put it inside. Whichever way you look at it. Away from the Chelsea garage and the cycles I could never buy anyway. So who cared? Not Moms. She could dry up those tears 'cause they didn't do no good. Naw, I was on the inside. But that wasn't all. And it wasn't Moms' fault that she didn't know about the inside or what can happen to a guy here. Pops breaking his neck building walls and then being kept outside. I couldn't tell her 'cause my lips was swollen.

But looking at her, I could tell she was already older in the face than she really was. And looking at her made me realize what had happened to me and how I was somebody different then. Somebody she was afraid to know. The feeling I had started up again as I was about to leave the visiting room. I thought my eyes was playing tricks on me and shit. Like I was high and the pounding in my head was making everything bent out of any shape or sound I could recognize. They saw me. I knew he was a friend of Metro's. I could tell by the way he looked at me. He had a woman with him and black guys from the inside talking with them. The thing was that I had to walk past them to get out, to get away from Moms' shrieking at me like I was something she was afraid of. Like her crying out about the chances I never had could help me any when I was trying to tell her with just my swollen eyes and lips and no words that I took my chance, shit, and look what I got.

Nobody helped. Not even the guards. Then he said something to me. She said something to me. And the two black guys from the inside just looked at me like my face and name was burning into their minds, just like my head was burning from the pounding blackness all around it. Lips and eyes. Lips calling in my mother's voice, "Chance? Christ Jesus! He ain't never had a chance." She had said the same thing at night court when they brought me in by myself, and she kept on saying it when the cops brought in the others and we had to stand in front of the night judge and get arraigned for murder. I hated that voice. It never shut up. No wonder Pops wanted to build walls all the time or work in other peoples' homes. He had to get away from that voice. I bet he heard the leaves, too. Didn't he? The goddamn leaves keep falling, and they lay on the ground in a dry spell even longer than they're supposed to. Everything's a bitch. Ain't nowhere to hide. Not even from the things you thought you forgot a long time ago. 'Cause they come back, just like the leaves come back. And when you on the inside, you remember everything.

"I have a friend, Lonny."

"So what."

"Don't you want to know about him?"

"Naw, man."

"He's black."

"Shit."

"What's wrong with that? Where I come from there are black people everywhere. We're the ones in the minority."

"Where's that?"

"Louisiana."

"Huh?"

"Louisiana. Lafayette County. You all don't know about it up here."

"I never heard of it."

"I came East to go to school. I'm a newspaper reporter now."

"I never read the papers."

"You want to come up for a drink? Some coffee? Coke? It's pretty hot out here."

"Naw."

"Is this what you call Indian summer?"

"October? Guess so. Sometimes, anyway. Why do you ask me these things?"

"I want to know about them. Why do they call it Indian summer?"

"I don't like you talking to me."

"Why do they call it Indian summer?"

"I don't like—shit, man. I don't know. 'Cause it's red. That's it. It's red."

"You're scared, aren't you?"

"Scared of what?"

"Me."

"Shit, man. You the one fucked up. What I got to be scared of?"

"Everything."

"Shit," I said, trying to walk away.

He kept looking at me. He wanted me to say something more. I didn't like him talking to me like that. I didn't know what to say.

"It's hot as hell out here," he said.

"You ought to know."

"Like I said. It's hot as hell out here."

"Don't talk to me no more. I got nothing to say to you."

"You can call me Metro. You can use my name, at least."

"Why don't you leave me alone?"

"Say 'Metro.' "

"Leave me alone, Metro."

"Why don't you leave *me* alone?"

"I'm waiting for my friends. Cuddles works around here."

"Then I'll stay."

"Suit yourself. I'm going somewhere else."

"You'll come back. Someday, all in leather and denim."

"You're crazy."

"Aren't you going to kiss me good-bye?"

"Shit."

He was crazy. But I didn't kill him. And when that black guy in the visitors' room started yelling at me and the pounding in my head got louder than I could stand, all I could do was hold my head with both hands and find my way back inside. His words were metal. My head ached. My lips was swollen so bad I couldn't say nothing back, only curl them up and grunt. This place makes you an animal. Then Moms' yelling and crying and his yelling and cursing. Nothing would go away. Shit. Shit. Shit. What the fuck's gonna happen to me now? Someone asked me later why I was there, inside, and I told him. He was in for a long time, too. Maybe longer than I was. I didn't know his name and when he looked at me, he acted surprised that I could be one of the guys 'cause I was so young-looking maybe. I didn't talk to him again. Not after what he said when he asked me, "You in for murder?"

"Yeah," I told him.

"You gonna fry for it, baby," he said.

My stomach suddenly went empty, the muscles got loose and watery. "Then again, maybe you won't," he said, acting like he had all the answers. Shit. I hated even more him saying "baby" like that. Like he was sorry. Who the fuck was he having pity on me? I didn't need it. Not like that anyway. I didn't know his name. Maybe what he said wouldn't even matter.

"Metro wasn't nothing to you. Why'd you kill him? Why?" the black guy yelled.

"Jesse, shut up. Calm down," she said, reaching for him and yanking him into the seat.

The two black guys from the inside just looked. At me.

"Leave me alone, Ruella. That guy's the one. Him and his friends. Why'd you have to kill him? You think you a man now? You think you a fucking man now?"

"Jesse, Jesse."

"Leave me alone, Rooms."

I got back inside. The guard closed the door loud and tight. The echo made me want to laugh. My lips were too swollen to move.

Naw, it wasn't 'cause I wanted to be a man. I was a man already. My head kept aching and I held it in both hands. I was a man already. That faggot Metro had nothing to do with it. But I couldn't say anything. Not even to Moms, who'd want to know how I was feeling. She was the one that counted for me. I wanted to tell her about Pops, why he built so many goddamn things. He built them good, to stand for a long time. But he could never visit the houses after he painted them or fixed them up. He must have known about the free fall of leaves and branches in a storm, the storm now repeating in my head. I wish I could've told Pops just how it felt being on the inside. I looked for him and saw only Moms and Patty.

"Moms," I tried to say.

"Christ Jesus! Christ Jesus!"

The black guy was some maniac. Yelling at the top of his lungs. The guard hustled him back to his seat. The girl tried holding him. My head still pounded with the echo of what he was saying and what Moms was saying and the guard trying to lock the door between us and that guy trying to jump all in my face screaming "Murderer! Killer!" like I was the only one feeling Metro's ass or making him go under. Ain't that what Metro told me himself? That he goes under? What the fuck was that guy trying to prove? That he's a man even though he fucks another man? Shit. Who wants to know that? The guards caught him, though. And I watched, smiling. I saw the girl again and the two black guys from the inside watching me watch her. They was all watching me. The black guys staring like they could tear off my skin. My head pounded again. I bit my lip to stop it. They kept looking at me. I tried to say something. Something to show that I never called them nigger. That was Cuddles and the others. I never called them nigger, so why don't they leave me alone. My swollen lips just grunted, made me feel like I was the animal they said I was. "Murderer! Killer!" Shit.

I went back to the cell and laid down. There was nothing else to do until they took me someplace else. Some other room far away from Moms and the falling leaves. Some other window to look out from and laugh 'cause you was away from all of them. But then you start remembering things again. Things you need to forget. You remember what got you here as if it was just yesterday. The only other thing to do is think about little things and wait for them to happen, like eating food or washing up. Some guys exercise alone or with others out in the yards. I'd go out, but I don't want to run into Cuddles and the others before they can get me out of here and somewhere safe upstate. They ain't alone, though, like me. And I wouldn't be alone if it hadn't been for the fight, which is all I got on my mind. But I remembered he called her Rooms once. Something like that. A funny name. Like Metro. Maybe it means something I'm supposed to know about. See how you get to thinking about stupid shit when you're inside? You hear me, Pops? Being inside ain't shit. There ain't nothing to do but wait. And all you can do is wait.

Then you start asking yourself silly shit. Like, would things have turned out this way if you was someone different? Or would you do it the same if you could start all over? We all want changes, I guess. Sometimes we think we could have done things differently. 'Cause we really think we can be different people than who we are. Would I have gone with that guy Metro and let him suck me or even fucked him since that's what he wanted? Would I have taken over Pop's work after he died and lived somewhere different? Could you imagine me getting a truck and painting a sign on it saying Antonio Russo and Son: Painting, Carpentry, Home Repairs? And maybe he wouldn't have worked himself so hard if I had shown some interest. At least not worked himself to death building things away from us. Saved up some money 'cause I was helping, see, and he could get us a house out there in Westchester like the ones he painted and repaired, and Moms could join the Garden Club and subscribe to *Newsweek* and *House Beautiful*. My sister Patty could take the yellow school bus and even graduate from a high school that had a swim team and cheerleaders and Saturday football games. And I'd be in school too, even playing on the teams and working with Pops for the summer like I did once, and we'd all be together.

Like the time he asked me to help him out on Saturday. Just go out with him to clean up after a job. It was ten dollars. I had nothing else to do. I went, but instead of helping like he wanted, I roamed all over that house. All ten rooms. And Pops had painted the whole inside. I imagined how we'd live there, me playing ball in front of the garage, running down the quarter-mile driveway to get the mail out of a gray metal mailbox with a flag. I'd have a dog, no, two dogs. Maybe pretend to go hunting in the woods out back. And Moms would call me in around six for supper. Pops would come home from the office with the evening paper

and we'd sit around the fireplace and sing Christmas carols
with hot apple cider or chocolate to drink and the snow
storming outside, away from us. Out there. Outside. Out of
that fucking room and out of my fucking mind. Shit. What
the fuck was happening to me? No snow at the window.
Just gray December. Early nightfall. Streets smelling like asphalt and fresh dogshit. Gasoline fumes. Roach spray. And
Pops' angry voice telling me, "Stop dreaming, kid. Clean
up. That's what you're here for, ain't it?" Cleaning up. In a
few hours, time to go home. My ten dollars. Throw out the
empty paint cans, the scraps of dingy wallpaper. It's time to
go home. Time to go inside to the greasy hallway and a
window view of bricks and soot and night as thick as nigger
hair. That's when I woke up. Pops. You hear me? We never
went back there. We never even had a place close to what
that was. A house. A simple, goddamn house. We never went
back for tea or tennis, never for Halloween trick-or-treat or
Sunday dinner, except once when we drove through White
Plains and you pointed to houses on both sides of the road—
it was a winding country road—saying, "I painted that pink
house there," and "See that garage? I fixed that," and for
another one, "Last year. Outside job." And I asked you,
"What about the inside, Pops?" And you wouldn't say nothing. Nothing. 'Cause we couldn't go back there. You couldn't
get back inside to show us what you'd done. Could you?
Naw. We saw only the outside of the houses, Pops. From
the inside of the car you drove. But Moms was smiling,
saying, "See what nice work you father does," and she was
moving closer to him and like a teenager, snuggling her head
under his free arm as he drove. Patty started asking for ice
cream and a ride on the swings in the park. But I was asking
about the inside I'd once seen. Nobody wanted to talk about
that. And we never went back after my ten-dollar clean-up
job, did we? Later, I heard Pops telling Moms how they let
him in through the back door like he was some nigger and
not the Italian home contractor he was. Shit, that man was
an artist. Look at what he built. Look how many times people called him for free estimates on a neighbor's recommen-

dation. But he stayed on the outside, even when he painted or built things inside. And there I was remembering how he came home tired one night in the winter after fixing gutters outside all day. Moms put him right to bed. The next morning the ambulance took him away and he never came back. The new wall and countertop he made in our apartment was left unpainted. Like a fool, I waited for him to come back. I waited for the wall and countertop to get painted, until, as Moms told me later, I got the paint myself and brushed "Fuck you" in thick black letters all over the place. Moms was scared then for the first time. And she kept on being scared. She must have known then that I was lost somewheres. But all she said was, "Christ Jesus! My boy ain't never had a chance."

Then we moved to Manhattan. Lower Manhattan, where it was cheap. I had to take care of Patty while Moms worked. And when the guys in the neighborhood saw me and Patty playing, they'd call me a sissy and throw stuff at us. But then Patty started going to school and I went to school. By the time I was thirteen and had some hair under my arms and a dick getting thick as my voice changed, I put on track shoes and a leather jacket. Stole a switchblade and dared them to call me a sissy again. I told Moms I was doing things for myself from now on. "I'm self-employed," I told her. "Like Pops. I'm gonna use myself."

She looked at me. "You mean you gonna use yourself up."

"Don't worry about me."

"Christ Jesus. If your father were—"

"He wouldn't say nothing. He'd build another wall somewhere or paint the apartment again. That's what he'd do."

"We could have had a house," she said. "He always wanted one." And she looked away from me without a smile or nothing on her face. I knew I was gone from her mind. I was lost to her. Maybe lost to myself. But I was gonna work. I was gonna bring home some money. I just hated it when she asked me where it came from, that's all. Why my pants leg was always bloody from the meat I'd stolen from the supermarket and left for her in the refrigerator. She always had the questions. She never wanted to hear the answers. Not the real ones, anyway. So I lied. I made up shit so she wouldn't cross me off with that blank look and make me feel like I was some rotten asshole for trying to help out. Shit. So I started hanging out with guys I met. Cuddles and them. I wasn't no Mama's boy. No sissy. No faggot either. I just fucking missed my old man.

But you can't keep thinking about the past. Naw. You can't change it and you can't keep feeling sorry for things you did or things you didn't do. I mean even if Pops wouldn't tell me things about the family, if he was silent all the time, it was probably 'cause he was keeping in all the anger from people he worked for and looking at the crummy neighborhood we lived in. I could have said stuff to him, told him things I was feeling. I could have started conversations or put my arms around his shoulders so he'd know I was thinking about him, that I cared how he felt coming back nights when Moms was just too tired to help him rest. I could have held his hand even and told him he didn't have to work at home too. He didn't have to build things for us. I loved him anyway. I could have told him that. Maybe then he wouldn't have worked and worked himself so, or built so many walls and cabinets and shelves, then painted and repainted the same damn apartment so many times. I could have helped him. But shit, I was in the streets. More so after he died. It was all too late. And I didn't have to build any walls, they just grew up inside me like a fucking cancer or the clap that wouldn't go away. And Metro? He thought he could stop the cancer maybe. All he did was make it grow worse. 'Cause there was something inside me I couldn't get rid of. Maybe I'm gonna die from it.

Can't keep thinking about these things. Not on the inside where all you do is wait. Waiting for transfers, waiting for food, waiting for hot water to shower, waiting for visitors, waiting for any day that's different from the day before. Waiting for your luck to change. Waiting for a trial and then

a verdict. Waiting for the end of your bid. Waiting for the
good times again. Waiting to get high off the memory of
some pussy or herb. Waiting for night and the streets filling
up with women strutting ass in jeans. Waiting for the right
moment to say, "Hey, sweet Mama" and have her give the
look that says, "I can give you something you ain't had in a
long time." Waiting to get inside her. Waiting to see each
other again. Waiting for a job that pays some money. Waiting in line for a movie and when you sit back all you see on
the screen is the slow playback of all those years, and you
feel like a fool for waiting this long, so you wait for the end.
And you wait for the end.

Shit. I had to do something before I lost my mind.
Exercises. Yeah. Sit-ups. Push-ups. One-two-three-four-
five-six-seven-eight, one-two-three-four-five-six-seven-
eight. Inhale. Exhale. Sweat on the floor. Sweat on my hands
now, pulling at the bars. Sweat making everything slippery,
even my words sliding out on tears: "Let me out of here,
please. Let me out of here. I wasn't the only one. I WASN'T
THE ONLY ONE."

And the walls answer you back.
"Shut the fuck up. I'm trying to read."
"Tell that white boy to shut his trap."

Brrrrrrrrriiinnnnggggg. A bell.
I got up from the bed. Must have been asleep. Cells
opened automatically. People came by with towels and
soap. Shower time. Not much hot water. My turn. Soap?
Yes. Towel? Yes. Now lost in a single file moving toward
steam and sweat. Hot water. A calm for sweaty arms and
hands and legs and ass crack. Then a hand grabbing at
my neck. A voice I suddenly knew. "That's what you get
for squealing, Lonny. We'd be free now if it wasn't for
you."

"Don't give me that shit. The cops had me, yeah. But
they knew it wasn't only me."

"How?"

"By the way you fucked up Metro, that's how. One

person couldn't have done all that. They knew it. I didn't have to say anything."

"But you told them where we was, Lonny. You shouldn't have done that."

"What do you care, Cuddles? You guys had gone when I looked around. You all left me right there. What would have happened to me? You didn't care nothing about me."

"Bet you won't open your mouth no more."

"Lay off me, man. I'm getting out of here, anyway."

"You lying."

"Naw, I ain't. I'm getting transferred. I'm going to some juvenile home somewhere. You'll see. You guys have a record. I don't. They showed me your photographs when they brought me in. Before I even said anything they had you all nailed. The neighbors even knew who you was. Everybody knew something. Everybody except me."

"You didn't need to know."

"I thought you was my friend, Cuddles."

"Shit."

"I thought we was tight."

"Shit."

"Now I'm the faggot, huh, Cuddles? I liked you, man. I trusted you."

"Shit."

"Now get the fuck out of my face."

I lost him as the line of prisoners I was in approached the shower. Steam was everywhere, like a wall with four sides. Cuddles must have been in it somewhere. Out of the corner of my eye I thought I saw him talking with Maxie and Lou, or guys who looked just like Maxie and Lou. I couldn't tell. The steam made everything look the same, but weird. But then I felt cold and empty inside right before I entered the steam and followed the sound of rushing water. I got chilled. And then I saw coming close to me those two black guys, both naked, that I remembered from the visitors' room talking to that girl they called Rooms and the guy they called Jesse who was yelling at me, "Murderer! Killer!" and I remembered Moms' voice in the background where I left her whining on Patty's shoulder and shaking her head like none of this was true and really happening to her. The black guys looked at me like they knew who I was. They hurried away like I stank. Maybe they really didn't see me. Who knows? But I was still cold as I got close to the shower and was already shivering when I entered the steam and the soft, hot water. I scrubbed myself clean, lathering soap everywhere, rinsing, lathering, rinsing. My skin squeaked 'cause all the shit was coming off me. I felt clean. Real clean. Locked away from the outside, enclosed in steam, naked of everything except some feeling you sometimes get standing with other naked men. The first thing you cover is your balls, then your eyes if you're lucky enough to move that fast.

Steam on your skin could feel like a new set of clothes. You didn't worry about seeing too much, but you started to hear differently. You could hear the water gurgling each time your feet or other people's feet moved. You could hear the quiet too. The end of the hot water? No more showers? You could hear the steam settle on tile. Then one by one the shower heads turned off. Like on signal. End of shower period. There'd be a bell soon. Some BRRRIIINNNGGGGG sound to send us back to the block. It'd be coming soon to make us dress and haul ass back to cinder-block rooms. Any moment. I still had time before the bell. Like we was naughty children and had to be told to go to our rooms. Shit. Then laughter. Voices of grown men, not children. Steam now and silence settling like a cat's paws on tile. My shower head was still on. A single jet of warm water. If it wasn't the end of the hour, then what was it? My hair was still wet, the lather dripping onto tiles, my feet feeling slippery and loose. A hand? Was that a hand on my back? Suddenly no water from above. Someone had turned off my shower.

"Hey man, I ain't through showering yet."

"Well, you through now." It was a black voice.

"Yeah, he's through." A white voice.

"We couldn't wait no longer." A sneering voice. Someone about to laugh. "Huh, fellahs?"

"No, I ain't through," I said. But I couldn't really see

anyone. I could see hair though, and some eyes. Then, as more steam settled, I saw mouths, beards, hands reaching through the air like they was lost. Bodies getting close to me. Closer. Voices like knives cutting through the steam.

"I ain't had my nut today."

"Ain't had mine in a long time."

"I'm gonna get me a nut. Don't you want a nut?"

Bodies too close. Steam cooling with weight on my shoulders. Hair dripping. My toes tried to grip the tile. Another hand in my face. I slapped it back. Again. I pushed out and away. Tried to move through the bodies, the smell of men, open mouths, open legs, cocks hard as clubs at my sides.

"You gonna be nice and let us get a nut?"

"What you talking about? Let me get by."

"He wants to get by, fellahs. Make room. Act nice, now."

"Yeah. We gotta act nice."

Suddenly a hand on my arm. I brushed it away again. Another. Another. Arms and legs holding tight. So tight I couldn't move.

"You better relax, sonny."

"Let me go."

"It'll be better for you if you relax. Act nice and you won't get hurt."

"Let me go. Let me go."

"He ain't acting nice, fellahs."

"Don't let him scream."

"Huh—" But I couldn't finish. A hand slapped against my mouth and held there. The whole palm tight. Calves next to my calves, hairy chest on my back. Stick of flesh at my waist, then hips, and moving down, down, down. Pushing in. Pushing in some more. The pain. Pain. Pain breaking me and entering. Someone threw my back forward, my hips up and out. Then I was down on tile and pushing away and slipping on the wet floor and trying to yell but couldn't make a sound. Everything in me was open. I heard my own voice somewhere saying, "Help me. Help me."

I remembered darkness. The darkness taking over the

gray steam. I thought of pearls, gray pearls and blankets. Then red as something started wetting me all over and seeping from me like from a torn place inside. It was red, all right. Red October leaves. Copper-brown November leaves. Hands from everywhere falling, falling onto me, into me. Rushing, pushing inside. Into me. I was open everywhere. The last voice was a tongue in my ear, "You got to relax, baby. My bid for breaking and entering ain't for nothing. I just want to get a nut."

"Hold him till I get mine."

"And mine."

"And mine."

I thought about the girl in the abandoned hallway and the twenty dollars we gave her. I had been in Cuddles' denim then. Riding her on the feet of roaches, too. Getting in. Getting off. The smell of pussy and Cuddles' denim armpit. The man on top was grinning at me, his teeth black and yellow in the cooling steam. Arms twisted mine. Opened my thighs wider and wider. The hand on my mouth eased off. I could breathe. I could look at what he was doing. I told him his name was Cuddles.

"My name is Jack, man."

"Tell me your name is Cuddles, man."

"Nobody here but me. And my name is Jack. Jack."

"Tell me it's Cuddles. Cuddles."

"Shit, man, you crazy or something?"

The air turned colder than before. I couldn't move from the tile floor. Steam like icicles settled on me everywhere. Cold needles. I found my voice again. "Does it feel good to you, Cuddles? Is it good to you, man?"

"Look at this shit. You bleeding, boy. You bleeding like hell."

I woke up in the prison hospital. My legs were tight and spread apart in metal clamps like I was some bitch about to have a baby. I must have been a bitch. They got their pussy, didn't they? Faggot pussy. They didn't care: Pussy is pussy, a nut's a nut. They would find any way to crack it. I tried to move. One foot, then another. Fine. But not the whole leg. Pain sliced through me like a knife tearing up from my thighs and ass and something warm and smelly oozed out of me like I was having a period or something. But the blood smelled like shit and I couldn't move to see how bad it was. My ass was swimming in it. My stomach queasy. There was blood on me like those red hands in October, those red leaves with a voice. I couldn't gather them in now or hold in anything. I was open from the inside, couldn't cover myself no more. I tried to hold things in again. I couldn't. Shit and blood again. Red September lips, red October leaves. Hands with knives of November like old copper. You know why they called him Metro? He was under, like I was. And I told him, if he could even hear me from somewhere else, "You think you got me now, huh? Metro, you think I'm the pussy now?" Shit. Christ Jesus! I never had a chance.

Jesse

What was Ruella pulling me into but more commitment? The prison was gruesome. It was too real. Phillip had a weight on him that showed through his eyes. And he probably saw too well what I was and what I was carrying. In prison he had to know how men could need each other.

The ride back to the city was long. First a crowded bus leaving Rikers and then a subway to midtown. I told Ruella I had to be alone. Just for a while. I'd go back to West 4th Street and face the bare white walls. No dance posters. No calendars. Maybe this time I wouldn't hear Metro's voice or the soft gurgles of our lovemaking there. But the memory that seizes you and wrings all the sweat from your nightmare is never the one you expect. All the guilt in your life creeps back as if you never fully explained the stolen cookie or the loose change taken from your father's desk top, and there's no one to blame but yourself.

I remembered traveling south with my mother on a train. Her mother had died and she was taking Charlie and me to the funeral. We traveled at night and changed trains in the middle of somewhere in the South where the darkness and the heat and steam from the tracks colored the trip like a nightmare. The next day in the bright sunshine of Irmo, South Carolina, it was even hotter. My brother and I waited in an open car while relatives filed inside a gray-wood country church. I could hear the preacher praying, then someone shouting. Everyone inside seemed to be crying. I heard my mother cry. I knew it was her voice although I couldn't see her. Her crying then had the same scratchy sounds as the ones she made when arguing with my father left her in one corner of the bed, nursing her eyes and swollen cheeks. The sound of tears always takes me back to Irmo and back to Connecticut where I was born. The years exchanged themselves within the same pain, from listening as my grandmother was eulogized to hearing my mother's muffled caution beneath distraught whimpers. Over the years those sounds returned to me as if my mother and I once shared a language no one else could use. Not even Metro, when I told him about my first trip South.

I tried saying things with her clothes. Touching, then wearing them. The feel of nylon on my skin was electric. I'd go into the bathroom when everyone had left the house and search through the hamper for any discarded dress, bra, stockings, or scarves. I wondered how girls grew to fill them with the softest flesh. I tried old socks and underwear. Then I danced.

The full-length mirror was my audience. In small, graceful steps, sometimes even curtsying as if before a gentleman partner, I'd dip and whirl the dress as fast and as far as I could, with the wide hems flapping against the sink, tub, toilet. And when I felt most fully the woman or young girl I had become so magically, I'd dab just a little rouge on my lips and cheeks to accent the natural redness under my skin. And I'd dance again and again until sweat streaked my brown face like an African mask, and I'd stutter in short whimpers of pleasure in a voice not even my own.

When I heard the car approach the driveway I'd quickly undress and flush the toilet to make believable sounds. While my mother unloaded the shopping, I'd return the clothes to the hamper and douse my face with water and cold cream. But another time, I learned later, someone was blocking the driveway and my mother had to park on the street. When she entered the house she must have heard the whirling dress and my whimpering song, my feet shuffling in the limited space of tile. She knocked furiously, her voice freezing my motion. "Jesse? Jesse, you come out of there. And make sure you put them clothes back right. I'm tired of finding my things all wrinkled and torn up. Come on, now. I got my washing to do."

My legs went stiff, my arms trembled, but the dress kept whirling in its centrifugal force of cotton and silk. I found my breath again and disrobed quickly. Without a word I slipped out the back door and ran for the playground. The neighborhood kids looked at me funny and backed away. I had the whole set of swings to myself. When I accidentally brushed at my face, some of the rouge came off on my arm. I'd forgotten to wash! The sudden distance of my friends became too clear. I looked away from them, trying to imagine how high the swings could take me.

That Halloween I dressed as a pirate, and my friend from junior high, Michael, who preferred to be called Micki, dressed as a girl in full calico skirt and loud orange lipstick. Charlie and I met him at the corner store once we had visited the houses on our side of Fairview Avenue. He joined us for the other houses but everywhere we went people recognized Micki, not us. My pirate's bandana and eye patch and Charlie's Dracula cape went unnoticed.

"That can't be Micki, chile," someone said.

"Ooooh, look how fine Micki is."

"He shore look good. Don't he look good?"

"Watch him strut his stuff. Go on, chile."

But they always gave us more candy than the simply dressed kids who came later. At one house where Micki modeled his calico and stuffed bosom we each got a Hershey bar—the five-cent size—and an apple.

At the end of Fairview we met Charlie's friend Al, but when Al spotted Micki he said under his breath that Micki was such a fox that he had to talk with him. The four of us settled in a nearby parking lot to examine our bags of treats. Al came up to Charlie and me. "You watch me handle this," he said. "Just you watch me." I took off the black eye patch and saw Al and Micki sitting on a log. Nothing happened. I went back to my apple and chocolate. Then out of the corner of my eye I saw a hand move, and I looked straight at Micki

who was caressing Al's thigh. I looked at Charlie. I said
nothing. And Charlie, who was also looking in that direction, said nothing. Al got closer to Micki and put his hand
on Micki's covered knee. Then his hand seemed to disappear.
Micki kept caressing Al's leg as if nothing had happened. Al
looked about nervously. We said nothing.

Then Al got up from Micki's side and went behind a
nearby truck. Micki straightened his skirt and followed.
Charlie and I remained seated. I listened and tried to make
the Hershey bar last longer by eating each square at a time.
I couldn't stop listening.

"Just let me wet it," Micki was saying.

"Naw, baby. I want it like this."

"But darling, I'd rather have it like this."

"You scared it's gonna hurt? It ain't gonna hurt."

Charlie shifted in his seat and moved away from the log
and the dim shadow of the truck. I remained seated. I was
glued to their sounds and the racing of my nerves. The candy
in my belly churned uncertainly. The chocolate became vol-
atile.

"Don't you like it this way?" It was Micki's voice again,
strained, less sure of itself, and thick with saliva.

"Just relax. It ain't gonna hurt."

"But . . . but . . ."

"Look here, punk. You wanna be a bitch, you better act
like a bitch. Now pull them panties down."

Just then Charlie called me away. He called me again.
Some invisible, strong arm held me to the log, listening and
imagining Al's hands on me. Charlie called me again and I
came away from the groaning shadow of the truck. But
Charlie didn't know then, and neither did I, that I would
spend half my life wondering what was happening behind
that truck and wanting whatever it was to happen to me.

I found out sooner than I expected.

The next summer I wore shorts and sandals bravely. I
found a place in the park where I could read. Once a car
circled the area near the bench. I caught the driver looking
at me from behind the wheel. I stared right at him. He sped

off. Minutes later he returned. I stopped reading. He asked
if I'd like to take a ride somewhere to get a cold drink. I said
yes. We talked. He brought me to a furnished room. We
talked some more.

"How do you want it?" he said.

I said nothing.

"You want it big? Big like this?"

The word squeezed out of me. "Yes."

"Where do you want it?"

"All over, I guess. Will it hurt?"

"It'll feel good. Lie back. Relax."

Cautiously. First my chest, then hips, thighs, I climbed
up on him, then under him.

He looked at me. "You don't really want it, do you?"

"Yes, I do. I want it."

"Where do you want it?"

"I want it in, all the way in."

"You don't want it bad enough."

"Please."

"Taste it."

"Huh?"

"You got to want it bad enough to taste. Crack your
jaw, baby. And when I'm ready you can crack your ass."

I didn't even know his name.

In another room at another time, with someone I thought
I knew, I learned a different dance. He threw a yellow silk
scarf at me. I tied it about my head, then tied it around my
waist. He smiled. "I want to see how much of a woman you
can be," he said, almost laughing. I looked hard at him. He
wasn't smiling.

I tried to laugh. "You got to be kidding."

His face went blank, his words like nails. "I want to see
how much of a woman you can be."

"What am I supposed to do?"

"Dance with it," he said, pointing to the scarf.

"Dance?"

"Dance till I tell you to stop."

He held himself in at the thighs. I took the square of

yellow silk and circled the air with it, wrapped it around my waist and threw it back into the air as I turned and whirled and the scarf dipped and whirled like the sun in a storm. My arms flailed before it, around it, my legs bending and pointing straight. I whirled and turned and whirled again.

"Faster," he said, his face contorting away from me. I could see him strain.

"Look at me," I called to him. "Look, look, I'm dancing. Dancing."

His hands went deeper into his thighs. He pulled at himself and his face showed every line of concentration. The eyes flashed open and shut, open and shut, the hands still digging and pulling in his pants. "Dance," he said again, almost to himself. "Dance, you bitch. You black son-of-a-bitch."

I spun and landed in a heap on the floor. But my head kept spinning away from me, away from my shivering legs. I drew my knees together and held myself in tight. I remained on the floor until he left the room without even looking back.

I telephoned home, long-distance. My mother's voice was as gray as her hair now. I asked if she had really wanted a girl. She said no, she hadn't wanted a girl.

"Then why did you give me your name?"

"Jesse's in the Bible. It's a man's name. My name isn't your name. Don't blame your troubles on me."

"But our names are the same."

"I'm Jessica. You're Jesse. You're a man. Act like one."

Before I said good-bye, I asked her to wish me luck for the audition. After a pause, she wished me luck. I eased the phone back to the receiver. I did my exercises alone.

The next morning, I called Ruella as promised and we met for lunch. We then went to her place to plan our audition piece. We took the Broadway #1 local uptown. The train was late. Usually you could count on the local coming every five minutes or so on a good day. The express trains sometimes took longer. I wanted to get going quickly, so I moved to the express side of the tracks at 14th Street. When nothing came, I turned back to the local side. Ruella followed my every move. I planned to go back to her place for a few minutes, gather the few clothes I had left there, the leotards and tights, and return home for good. The closeness between us was grating. I needed her more than was good for either of us. I didn't say anything, just smiled at her, and she smiled back. A small crowd had gathered by the tracks. Soon the train screeched in, *caroom-boom-clack, caroom*. An express, finally. Only one of the two doors opened. We piled inside and found seats near an air vent or a heater, you never could tell which.

As soon as the train left the station, the lights inside the car started to flicker. The car ahead of us went dark, then our car and the car behind us. After a moment the lights came back on in the same sequence. Mini-blackouts in a speeding hulk. A well-dressed man got on at Penn Station, 34th Street, and as soon as the car doors shut he opened his briefcase and pulled out a Bible. He started to preach, brandishing the book like a weapon. No one paid him any mind, and he left our car for the next, following the succession of blackouts all through the train as if the Word itself were guiding our travel. Ruella and I burst out laughing. I was sure the man was headed to a midtown insurance office somewhere forty stories high, and he was getting ready for his imminent ascent to heaven.

Suddenly the train stalled. The lights went out. Air stopped coming from the vent. All was still. I started to sweat although it wasn't that hot. I was about to stand up when the train lurched forward and lumbered into the next station. The waiting riders looked angry. Ruella moved in closer to me and took my hand. Crowds squeezed onto the train. The door wouldn't close. "Get the fuck off the doors," said a voice over the loudspeaker. The door groaned shut. The train pushed itself out of 42nd Street, accelerating for the nonstop ride to 72nd.

I kept thinking about the visit to the prison. I'd think about anything just to keep my mind off the train and the other passengers. Ruella's hand squeezed mine and I smiled at her, but her look said she was clinging to me again, and I didn't want her to cling. We were already close. We danced. We took the subway. We visited the prison. We saw Phillip. I felt his blood boiling beneath the skin and felt my own blood freeze. He looked at me with the same suspicion my father did when it took me so long to learn how to ride a bike, or when I preferred to shine shoes for a quarter downtown, or fuss about my mother's hair when she would let out the rollers and toss the newly formed curls carelessly about her head. I wanted to care for those curls. I hated baseball and marbles, and even when I was a paperboy once I learned to ride a bike, I'd fold each paper neatly and place it perfectly in whatever piece of property it belonged. Charlie watched me suspiciously, like my father did. Like Phillip, as if the careful rolls of newspaper could never hide the telltale flutter in my walk. I was a sissy. And they all knew it before I did. And I was trapped longer than I cared to know in my mother's hamper heap of bras and panties and flowered blouses. Trapped in imitation silk and rosewater, with no exit from the mirror frosted with the breath from my dance. No doubt this was what Phillip saw in his suspicion, and this was probably what Ruella knew and feared, that the confused look of fathers or brothers made you realize you could love them more fiercely and more dangerously than any woman could.

There was danger in the subway lights, whizzing by. Suddenly the screech of brakes and a long wail echoing through the dark. We must have been around Lincoln Center, the West 60s, judging by the amount of time that had passed. The train stopped dead. People shifted about nervously. I was afraid. The lights went out. Burning metal and the sharp odor of electricity rose through the car. Smoke pricked at my eyes. A gravelly voice came over the loudspeaker saying something no one understood. The doors wouldn't open. The smoke got thick.

People coughed. From somewhere came jitters and laughs. A child started to cry. "Goddamn train," someone said. "Must be a fire somewhere."

"God, no," said Ruella, her voice raspy in my ear. She clung to me tighter.

That started the near panic. No one could move. I tried to stand. Legs jostled, bodies pushed and shoved. We could go nowhere.

I remembered the signs, "Subway tracks are dangerous . . . Follow the instructions of trains crews or police." But there were no police, no crews, no motormen, no instructions. The smoked curled into our clothes and cramped bodies.

A siren sounded. Lights flickered. The smoke was like a fog. A jolt of cold, crisp air came through the car. People separated, flowed. More smoke came. We had room now to move. I made Ruella get down on her hands and knees with me, and we crawled along the floor, crawled among crumpled papers, brown paper bags, chewing-gum wrappers. We went from one car to the next, crawling, sucking for air, fumbling blindly in a silent mass. We reached the last car and the door was open onto air and darkness. Then the flicker of more lights. People straightened up and moved toward the flickering lights. "Subway tracks are dangerous," I repeated to myself. Then louder, "Are you with me, Ruella?"

"Yes, Jesse, I'm all right."

From nowhere appeared a motorman with a lantern. He told us to stand up against the wall and follow the line of riders. Farther ahead was another lantern signaling the first. I felt another gust of air. It was an open manhole cover. One by one people inched up the hot metal rungs and went out into the bristling air. I pulled Ruella ahead of me and pushed her up the ladder from behind.

Outside there were police and fireman everywhere. Several ambulances stood by. I found Ruella's hand and held her close to me. Her eyes were red. Mine were red. "What happened?" I asked an officer next to me.

"Just a small electrical fire. Nothing big."

"Anybody hurt?" asked Ruella.

"None too bad."

"I'm glad we're OK" I said, holding Ruella again. She

looked at me, and I couldn't tell whether she was glad to be out of that tunnel and train and turmoil or glad simply to be in my arms.

"Thanks, Jesse."

"For what?"

"Leading me out."

"You found me, remember. In the warehouse. You pulled me from the splinters. And we danced."

"You were so calm, Jesse. It'll be a long time before I can take another train," she said.

That's when I knew I could leave her.

PART FOUR

Ruella 7

There was smoke everywhere on me. There was smoke all in my clothes and all in my hair, like I had a head full of burning wires. I tasted smoke on my tongue and teeth. My whole body felt smelly and thick.

We were lucky, though. Some people had to spend the night in the hospital. No one was killed, thank God. Truth is, I felt like it was the end of something I couldn't quite name. It took me two whole days to get my nerves back. When I had to go out, I took the bus. No subway was going to wreck my nerves. And not my last nerve, for sure.

Later, Jesse and I practiced without music. Then he bought the Nina Simone album and we practiced again. He kept humming the tune over to himself as we stretched together on the floor. I started to sing. He joined in. We halted at the pronouns. "He doesn't know his beauty. He thinks his brown body has no glory. If he could dance . . ."

"That song's about me, too," he said.

"And me."

We laughed.

The next day everyone was watching us during auditions. The call required two parts. First, an original dance with a partner, something like an improvisation, but which showed how you worked with another dancer. The second part was an individual execution of combinations given by the dance captain. If you passed the first you could present the second. Anna Louise thought we had a good chance with the Simone-Cuney piece.

"*She* doesn't know her beauty," I remembered. "She thinks her brown body has no glory. If she could dance . . . If she could *dance.*" I said this over and over to myself and imagined all the graceful movements that could come to someone like me who had to practice, to work at it, like Mama would say and Aunt Lois, too, before I left home. I was not a pretty woman. I didn't mind it, not really. You got to work for anything you want in this life. You got to dance.

Jesse moved with me. His body was leaner, tight. The leotard and tights no longer sagged at the folds of muscles he'd developed. I touched his head. He touched mine. I bent in plié and he lifted me high on relevé. My knees turned out in harsh precision. I was in the air briefly, his arms tight at my waist, his feet firm on the polished floor. The song continued. My whole body was an ear opening up to sound and movement, sweat and space. Simone, Cuney, Jesse, and me. I bent and opened. Jesse bent and opened. We were dancers simply dancing. I wasn't talking now in borrowed words, but in my own language of arms and hands, of delicate and expressive fingers, of head and waist and twisting torso. I told another story. Jesse answered with his movement connecting to mine as mine connected to his, and we circled through the words of song and light, airy motion. He told me in those arms and contractions of stomach, lifting chest and tight pirouettes, bullet jetés, that he could be a tree or a flower and still be strong, that his brown body had glory in movement, in music, even in the pain from somewhere deep that boys named after their mothers are different. I said I understood. His arabesque and grand plié told me that some boys take glory in their difference, have grace too, and the promise of wings. I extended forty-five degrees, then ninety. Which said, women too could be different and could fly. He angled closer. He called me Rooms for short. Rooms for all the spaces we created where he could dance to several tunes at once, then rest.

Later, I would let him touch me here and here, holding each breast and pushing tenderly between my thighs, on point. Point of finger, tongue. His wide hands would be copper autumn leaves falling around me and onto me, covering me as if I were the earth. I gathered them in from the cold. Jesse danced in my room. He called me Rooms. Phillip called me Lil' Sis and Lady, which I liked even more. Everybody called me something other than my real name. What was I going to call myself? How would I move in my own dance? "If she could dance. Naked under palm trees. She would know . . ." The song continued and I continued bending and opening and bending and opening. One-two-three-four. Two-two-three-four. Step five, bend six, leap seven, down eight. Hold, two-three-four. *Hold.*

Anna Louise thanked us again and said the list of accepted dancers would be posted on the First Company bulletin board in two days. I didn't think I could wait that long. Or sleep. My legs were still shaking long after Jesse and I came off the floor. He was sweating. After resting a moment, we were asked to join the other dancers who were following the dance captain's combination. I wasn't with Jesse at all this time. There were so many dancers following the combinations that I wondered who really had been selected. When I looked for Jesse in line he was standing next to another black dancer, a man. Something caught me inside and made my legs go heavy, plodding. The two of them danced in front of me and couldn't even tell I was watching. I tried following Jesse's steps and the dance captain's combinations, but I found myself watching Jesse and the other dancer more than the dance captain. I couldn't concentrate. Shivers shot through my legs and I thought I had a sudden case of shin splits. But it wasn't my legs at all. It was the handsome man dancing next to Jesse and pulling Jesse's gaze away from the dance floor and into his eyes. I was scared. Scared for myself. Scared for Jesse, too, this time. My stomach knotted itself, and each muscle pulled against the upward contraction I needed to lift my right leg high in extension. I fumbled through the steps, all the while watching Jesse smile at the other dancer and the other dancer smile back. They were

auditioning all right, but more for each other than for the
dance captain. The thought froze me from the inside out and
I just couldn't move right. Truth is, I was jealous.

Anna Louise called me off the dance floor. "What's the
matter, Ruella? I called you three times. Are you feeling all
right? Maybe you're too exhausted after the last piece."

"Yes, Anna Louise, I guess so."

"You even stumbled once. I was afraid you would fall."

"I don't understand it, either. I'm sorry."

"Perhaps you'd better rest."

"But what about the rest of the audition?"

"I'll try to talk to the choreographer. I'll do what I can."

"You think he'll give me another chance?"

"I can't promise anything."

"Wait. Let me get back in line. I'm all right now."

"Are you sure, Ruella?"

I found a place in line out of sight from Jesse and the
man next to him. I focused on each movement the dance
captain showed for the third time. I flung hips and arms
wide, turned out knees until they were flat as plates, pointed
my toes like the tip of a long brown knife. I leaped wide,
moving away from Jesse's range of vision as quickly as I felt
myself leaping into something of my own. I pliéd and ar-
abesqued grandly until sweat made my feet slippery on the
floor. But I kept on dancing and dancing. I knew every step
now and could add a little expression of my own. Something
with personality in it, something from the inside moving my
feet. I flowed into movement, lifted stomach, chest, head,
straight and higher than even Jesse could. My hands and feet
were feathers. Light as leaves. Then I noticed there were
only five dancers left with me on the floor. I danced again
and smiled with the movement; everything inside me was
light and thin and something new to present. I was the dance
and the room itself. There was no more space inside me.
Nothing more to hold in guardedly, unsure. No place where
anyone could enter so freely and violate with a touch or a
broken heart. I had no more room inside myself for that. No
more spaces to give. Everything was outside now, and mov-

ing through the studio like an express train through a local stop. This time I was full of movement, this time I knew where I was going.

Anna Louise smiled at me. She said again that names would be posted in two days. Some decisions were already made, others were pending. Some dancers would be seen for call-backs. But two days? Could I even wait that long? I headed for the dressing room but just then Jesse came up to me from behind as if to surprise me with something. He wasn't alone. I could hear the other man's voice before Jesse spoke to me. I turned away to ease off my leg warmers, and give the hint I was leaving, and only after a considerable pause did I finally say hello. Jesse introduced me to his new acquaintance: Rodney, Rodney Alexander. He smiled and Jesse smiled, but by then I had figured out that they were really smiling for each other, showing all teeth and lips, just like they were really dancing for each other, showing tight chests and thighs. Auditioning, my foot! I secretly hoped neither would pass into the First Company although they needed more male dancers than female. But just who was this new guy, this Rodney?

Jesse wouldn't say anything more about him. And I didn't ask too many questions. I wasn't that interested. Not really. But I did see them exchange telephone numbers, and in Jesse's silence later I could tell he was thinking about him. So I said, "Rodney *is* nice looking." And Jesse said, "He's all right."

"As a dancer, I mean. I think he's pretty good."

"Handsome," Jesse said, "And, yes, a good dancer."

"Think we'll make the company?"

"We'd better."

"Why?"

"Because I just had an idea for a dance. I'd like to choreograph something."

"What kind of dance?"

"A dance for men. Two men. A male *pas de deux.*"

I started to laugh, then caught myself. "It's been done before," I said.

"But it's always some version of the Icarus-Daedalus story. One dies, the other flies to safety. Or Cain and Abel. Two brothers. But still one of them dies. I want to do something about lovers. How two men can fly together and land safely, feet back on the ground."

"Sounds confusing to me."

"It'll be great."

"For you and Rodney, perhaps."

"Who's talking about Rodney?"

"I can read between the steps. Anyway, you two dance well together. Not that I was noticing or anything."

"You're bullshitting."

"No, I'm not, Jesse. But what about me? You've forgotten about me that quickly? I'm a dancer, too. And Metro, what about him?"

"He's dead. The dance is about him. Rather, us. What we could have been."

"And now Rodney?"

"Look, Rooms—"

"Ruella, Ruella McPhee."

"Listen, Ruella. He's asked me to visit later. For drinks."

"Then you won't be coming by my place tonight?"

"I hope not."

"Shit. You don't have to say it like that, Jesse."

"I'm sorry."

"You better stay there too, Jesse. At his place or yours."

"Huh?"

"I want to be alone for a while," I said. My lips felt thick. I bit into them to stop the trembling creeping all into me like the smoke. "I want to be alone," I said again, my lips almost swollen now, and chewy.

"Until tomorrow, you mean. Tomorrow, right?"

"No, Jesse. Longer than that."

"I see."

"I do too," I said. "Now."

Jesse's eyes were on my back, but I turned more fully away from him and walked alone outside the studio. My feet felt funny, lighter, and were leading me in a different direction from Jesse's. I carried nothing but my dance bag, and my shoulders felt light. I tried to get the first train I heard screeching into the station. Missed it. Another fifteen minutes pacing the platform. What in the world was I doing taking a train? Well, there I was. Then, for no reason at all, I started smiling to myself and smiling at other waiting passengers. I was learning new steps just pacing there and feeling the vibrations underfoot of the coming train. Truth is, I was practicing for the time I'd dance solo or not dance at all. And I had nothing at all to fear from fire.

For two days I cleaned my apartment myself. And when I returned to the studio, Lord, our names had been posted.

Lonny

hree weeks it took to get out of that fucking hospital. Three weeks of laying up looking at the blank pastel-green ceiling and the same four walls. Then another couple of weeks after that before I could take a shit without holding onto a guardrail because of the pain, or stop taking the fucking laxative to soften the shit so it wouldn't tear the lining of my ass and so the muscles in it could heal. All those weeks of bed and doctors and television. At least I had better food than the other inmates. And I didn't have to work on some bullshit farm for boys upstate. But they finally had me transferred there when we lost the trial. I guess I was the lucky one: hospital and upstate reform school. The others got sent to different prisons all around the state. The lawyer said the judge was easy on me 'cause I was the youngest and didn't have a record. And the jury believed me. I was guilty of being an accomplice, they said. But not of murder. So by the time I got to the reform school I had already done time in jail waiting for trial, and time in the hospital waiting for my ass to heal. When I got upstate there wasn't much to do except read and go to a few classes and do a few chores. I was taking mechanics training for a job when I got out because I knew something about cycles from hanging around the garage in Chelsea.

Once I was there for a while and on good behavior they gave me visiting privileges. Once a month I could go home. Moms was getting sick and Patty had to take care of her after school. That also helped me get leave. Soon, I'd be home for good. But I wasn't going near those meat-packing warehouses on West 12th, and I was staying away from Chelsea. Maybe I could talk Moms into moving back to the Bronx since she still had some friends there. Maybe I did, too.

The country is different from the city. And it wasn't until I was upstate long enough that I really thought about that difference. You forget things you want to remember when you're on the inside and counting cinder blocks to pass the time. But you remember shit you want to forget. In the country I knew I was cool. Not only because I came from the city but because I had left dead leaves and cloudy skies behind me on the endless concrete. There were no leaves in the hospital and no leaves following me upstate, just snow and chores to do like shoveling snow, cutting wood, and going to class for job training: cooking, auto mechanics, even drafting if you wanted. I didn't make many friends. How could I? I didn't want nobody to know what had happened to me at Rikers. They might get ideas too, thinking I was really like that, or that I really wanted things to happen the way they did. Like it wasn't even those white guys and black guys pumping into me and trying to kiss me, but in my mind it was one guy only, Cuddles. And they'd think I really liked that shit. The doctor did. He kept asking me questions about me and Pops and how we got along. I told him that Pops built things, that's how we got along. What kinds of things? he asked. Walls, I said. We got a roomful of walls. What kind of walls? Walls that have ears and eyes and big red lips. Walls that don't talk back and don't even touch you, but walls that get painted very, very often.

I didn't get what the doctor was driving at. He didn't get me either. So we stayed there quiet for a while, me with my legs up and open and my ass all swollen and sore trying to tighten itself back and at least control itself, and the doctor grinning down at me asking if I really wanted it that way and if that wasn't the real reason why I had held Metro's face to my groin while the others made him take it up the

ass. Shit no, I thought. But he kept asking me that and grinning, so by now I knew what he wanted. I said yes. Yes, I
wanted it that way. He stopped smiling. He wrote stuff on
his notepad. "That's fine," he said. "It's good to get it off
your chest." But I didn't have nothing on my chest. I just
wanted him to shut up about Pops and about me being one
of those guys who needed his touch or the touch of any man.
Then he left me alone. I thought about the pain between my
legs and the smelly guys who put it there and dug so deep
that I lost all control of blood and shit and even my feelings
inside. Damn, I said aloud. Damn. Damn. Damn. And there
I was still lying in it. It took time, but I got well. Got a light
sentence, too. The attack was proof enough for the judge,
lawyer, and jury that I was really different. But this doctor
was trying to make me more different than I was. Which is
why I had my own room at the boys' farm upstate. Something must have been in the psych report about how I wanted
it to happen the way it did, and how I must have wanted
Metro, too, all the while before they killed him or found
me lying in the chalk. I had a room to myself. They was
afraid I'd harm the others. Shit. I liked going solo. I was
good. I followed the rules. And I got to go home once a
month.

Which is how I learned about the quick bucks on 53rd
Street between Lex and Third. How much money you could
make just following along. I could use the money. It took
all my allowance to pay for the bus trip down and to try to
surprise Moms and Patty with a little something. My first
time out, I sat on the bus next to some guy who kept rub-
bing my legs the whole trip to the city. He was the one who
told me about the bars and corners on 53rd and how much
money he made. What the hell, I thought. Let some guy
blow me for twenty dollars, why not? That wouldn't mean
nothing since he was doing the blowing, not me. He was
asking me for it, with a crisp new bill folded in his hand. All
I had to do was sit in the car like I was waiting for a red
light or something. It was the simplest thing. But I was too
scared to do anything that first weekend out. I was sure I'd

get caught. When you already had a record, even the first one, you had to be more careful.

The second weekend free I made it to 53rd and Third. Just checking it out, see. I didn't say nothing to nobody. I just stood at the corner. I didn't even go into any of the bars. What for? I didn't have no money to spend on drinks. And I didn't know yet how to look like I wanted something to drink so the men who was buying would notice. I stayed outside, checking the whole scene out until it got cold. I stopped at a nearby coffee shop and had hot chocolate. I didn't expect nothing there. That's probably why I looked so relaxed and calm. But this older guy spotted me and sat down at the counter. He ordered a coffee. Black. No sugar. Before I knew what was happening, he pushed a folded note to me. I thought it was just paper and would have thrown it away, but it felt like money. It smelled green. A ten-dollar bill. Then he reached for my check and paid for both of us. I didn't know what else to do. I followed him outside.

Ruella

That spring of 1976 I looked forward to the coming dance concerts and theater festivals. Especially since I was with the Taylor Johnson First Company. We'd been in rehearsals all winter, doing warm-up stretches close to the radiators and with as many leg and body warmers as we could wear and still move around. I thought about Phillip who was getting out on parole. And I thought a lot about Jesse. In spite of all we had been through, he was still my friend. We still fussed like cat and dog, but I couldn't keep him and couldn't let him go.

After the trial in December, when the boys were found guilty of murdering Metro, Jesse returned to the apartment on West 4th Street. He fixed it up differently and he was living there alone, but he was dating Rodney, who hurt his ankle and wasn't cast in the show. Too bad for him. Truth is, I didn't care if Rodney got back into the company or not. I was dancing solo. Jesse got my message and left me alone. I didn't even miss him staying with me. We saw each other enough during rehearsals. Sometimes we danced together just to practice.

Jesse was luckier than I thought. He was asked to create a piece for a workshop presentation at City Center in May. He wouldn't talk about the piece except to say it was a dance for males. I figured as much. Something about brothers, maybe, or fathers and sons. Lovers, perhaps. He promised to show me some of the steps before the company director saw the whole thing. Up to now Jesse had been silent.

A little too cautious, if you ask me. They were at least giving him a chance. That was more than most dancers got.

I wrote Phillip to tell him Jesse and I broke up. He was sad for me at first, but he said he understood how a man like Jesse wouldn't stay with a woman long. I understood, too. That's why I wrote him about it. But I also wanted Phillip to know a man could be loved for his tenderness, not ridiculed or called a faggot. And Jesse was tender, most of the time. Phillip had a tenderness too, until it got too hard for him to show it and he had to cover it over with drugs. At least he could say he was high. Just high. Never lonely or afraid or just wanting to be loved. I wanted Phillip to know I could recognize that need in a man and not make fun or try to dominate him. Anyone. I saw the same feelings in myself. I knew it couldn't be weakness. "It couldn't last long, Lady. Not with a man like Jesse," he wrote. But what about you, Phillip? I wanted to ask. What about you? He said we could talk about it when he got out. He thought he'd be released in time to see me dance. And Jesse, too, if he came to both programs.

When I saw Jesse he didn't talk too much about himself. I had to ask questions, or guess. He didn't say much about Metro anymore, either. I didn't ask about Rodney. When Jesse did say something about the dance he was choreographing, he said he was watching men do different things to study their motion. He gathered his material, he said, from watching men strut with their ladies on Saturday nights or play basketball in the street, but I never thought that was his kind of movement. These are black men, he told me, dancing by themselves. And I said, maybe that's why I'm dancing solo, and to my own music. No black men to dance with.

One afternoon the phone rang just as I was returning from the office. It was Abdul. Yes, I remembered him. He said he was living in a halfway house out in Brooklyn. Could I meet him for dinner? Yes. Movies? Sure. But I told him before he said anything further that I didn't have any room at my place. I repeated my whole name, Ruella McPhee, and said how much I liked my name—all five syllables. You just can't squeeze them all into one like Jesse did, calling me Rooms.

"My name used to be Gerald," he said. "Gerald Washington, before I converted to Islam. Now my name is Ibrahima Abdul Assiz."

"What does that mean?"

"It's an Arabic name. For me, it means that I know who I am. I can choose my own name. Not what anybody else wants to call me, like Ger or Gerry or even plain Washington. Sometimes in prison you even start to hate math because the numbers say you're an inmate."

"I like Abdul."

"I like Ruella. There's a tune to it. Are you a song in disguise?"

"Sometimes. What instruments do you play?" I asked, laughing. And he laughed with me.

"I live alone, Abdul. I like it that way, at least for the time being. I need all my space."

"I know. Maybe I've already said too much."

"No, you haven't."

"I'm sorry if I have. I just wanted to see you again. I don't know that many people. Good people, like you."

"Thanks."

"Can I call on you again sometime?"

"Sure, I'd like that."

"So would I."

After that we went out a lot together. Abdul wanted to go everywhere: The Bronx Zoo, Central Park, the Bowery, even riding the tram to Roosevelt Island at night just to see the lights. "I love being outside," he said. And I could feel how much he enjoyed it. Then he took my hand and held it for a long time. The halfway house helped him find a job, and at night he studied Arabic. He had ideas about women, strict ideas. But I had ideas about men. I was a dancer, I could bend. I had had lots of practice. I told him that maybe

I could teach him a few things. He laughed at first. Then we talked. He was learning another language and moving in a different space. I felt good with him. I liked the sound of his name and the soft way he said "Ruella." I tried imitating his voice when I was alone or staying late at rehearsals.

The opening was in a few weeks. And Phillip would be out on parole soon. I was afraid he'd want to stay with me. When you have family you don't have to go to a halfway house. I was afraid of Phillip being that free. Truth is, I was afraid he'd be like Jesse and want all of my space, the space I was just beginning to share with myself and Abdul. Jesse filled that space with so many horrors I could barely breathe. Abdul showed me other spaces. Spaces inside. I still had a little time to think things through.

Before rehearsal one Saturday Abdul suggested we visit the Statue of Liberty. We left early in the morning to have enough time to climb all the way inside. I hadn't been there since I was a little girl in a crowd of summer tourists. The winding stairs inside the green metal gown seemed endless and huge, but this time the stairs were only wide enough for one pair of feet in a slow climb. Abdul climbed in front of me and held my hand, easing me up and around the narrowing spiral. When we neared the top to look out from the windowed crown, Abdul stepped back as if he had hit a wall. Then I felt it—a wall of heat that came from the sun beaming on the shut windows. "What heat," I said, pulling back.

"It's not just the heat," he said. Then he pointed to the Wall Street area and the twin World Trade Center buildings. All you could see were the thousand squares of windows towering up. "That's the view from the joint, too," he said.

"What do you mean?"

"Windows you can't open. From Rikers all you see are windows you can't open. Your own window and all the windows of Manhattan across the river. But you also see the bridges, and you hear planes taking off and landing at LaGuardia so you know people are going somewhere. But when you get outside all you see are windows. Windows that don't open."

"Exchanging one prison for another? It can't be that bad, Abdul." Then I thought about my return trip from Comstock State Prison last fall and how I noticed for the first time the locked gates on the windows of my building, especially the upper and lower floors. I was glad my windows had no locked gates. But Jesse looked out of them with the same trapped look I remember Phillip had when I'd seen him last. Jesse was different. It wasn't a question of windows or gates. He was trapping himself all the time.

"Let's get out of here," Abdul said, moving from the heat and the shut glass. He led me down the spiral stairs. I was afraid of missing a step and falling or twisting my ankle this close to opening night. Besides, I still had a rehearsal to make. We hurried to the ferry, and it didn't seem like Abdul took a full breath until we were nearing Manhattan and finally disembarking at Battery Park. Our hurrying put me a little ahead of schedule. We sat in the park and looked back across the river. The statue seemed small now and hardly important at all. Just somebody's tarnished rag baby doll.

Tarnished is exactly the way I began to see Jesse after that. Green and rusty brown. As soon as I arrived for rehearsal he started in on me, asking where I'd been for the past few hours he'd been calling on the phone. "Out," I told him. "I've been seeing the city from the outside." Another cat-and-dog fight was beginning. I didn't want him to hurt me more than he already did by giving Rodney so much of his time. But I hadn't expected that he would sound hurt too.

"With Sheik What's-his-name? He's probably got you walking three paces behind him."

"Since when do you care about names? Real names, I mean. You jealous?"

"Not another fight, please, Ruella. I just wanted to tell you about this dance. I've found the music for it. Ellington's 'Take the A Train.'"

"How original," I said, trying to turn away. "Then I know what your dance is about."

"Traveling," Jesse said, a little too quickly. "It's about moving from place to place."

"Rooms to rooms, you mean."

"What's gotten into you?"

"Nothing, Jesse. But you're still moving underground. You haven't changed at all. I was stupid to expect as much, huh?"

"Why stupid?"

"I was stupid to fall for you. It was a stupid idea. I'm over it now. You're seeing Rodney. I'm seeing Abdul."

"You happy?"

"Don't say it like that. You act like a person's not supposed to be happy. Well, yes, I'm happy. Some feelings you don't have to fight for."

"I'm glad for you, that's all."

"Don't condescend to me, Jesse. Not after all I been through."

"And me? What about me?"

"You never saw me, Jesse. I was just a place to come to. Metro was the same, only he was transportation. Traveling, you call it. Only you never arrived."

"Where was I supposed to go?"

"You never arrived at knowing who he was. Like he wasn't worth it, or wasn't good enough. And you know what happened?"

"What?"

"Metro stayed underground."

"I don't follow you, Ruella."

"You're not supposed to follow me, Jesse. I want you to listen to me."

"I'm trying. I really am."

"Maybe. But you know, Jesse, I caught on pretty quick. I wasn't going to let you do to me what you did to Metro.

You probably drove that boy to hate himself. Just like you tried to drive me. Metro couldn't live with you, because you made it hard for him to live with himself. He probably was looking all the time for some way to die. Maybe he wasn't strong enough to do it himself."

"Suicide?"

"Or self-hatred. It's all the same. He was traveling, all right. Right into the goddamn tunnel you trapped him in."

"You're cruel, Ruella."

"I'm honest."

"That won't happen to you? Ever?"

"Not with these thighs, baby. I found my way to the outside. I'm visiting places on my own. So, if you'll excuse me, I have to get ready for the next call."

He said nothing. He waited. He said nothing more. I turned back and started to leave. Jesse couldn't see my lips quivering or my knees weakening. I got to the ladies' room just before the tears came. But I didn't really cry. Not for real, anyway. Well, just a little. After a moment I joined the other dancers on the floor.

Truth is, I didn't have a solo part. Not really. I was just one in a group of girls. We all got carried in on the shoulders of a few male dancers. Jesse wasn't one of them. Rodney would have been if he hadn't twisted his ankle so badly. I wouldn't have minded Rodney carrying me in. Once across the floor we entered again on triplets, then held in alternate time. Arabesque. We made a circle that broke as soon as it was formed. On a second count of eight I did an extension. Right leg, then down. Left leg, then down. Light steps into a circle again, then hold. Each girl ran forward to join arm and leg with another dancer. We collapsed in a heap. We rose alternately, off the beat. Then a flurry of jazz. Coltrane's "A Love Supreme." As each woman rose, swayed hips, then arms, she appeared to be reaching offstage and stage-front for something at a distance, something out there to hold on to. Some were pulled up from the heap, others fell gracefully back down. Step-two-three, relevé. First one, then another.

Everyone was up. Hold-two-three. Extension: three o'clock, five o'clock. Someone at six o'clock. Hold. The men had gone. No one to carry us offstage. We continued to reach from inside ourselves, stomachs in contraction, for those things at a distance. The saxophone droned on, and on, and on. Lights dimmed. We held in relevé.

I was really trying not to feel sorry for myself. I was glad to learn new steps, even if I was dancing solo only in my mind. At least I was traveling in the light. Stagelight, yes. Artificial color, yes. But in movement with a kind of memory. Things you've felt or done before. Places you've been to. I thought I was really changing.

The first change had come when I found Jesse in the Village. That really frightened me, although I wasn't aware enough of the strength of that fear to say anything about it. Not to Phillip. Not to myself. I realized how fixed Jesse was. It wasn't just that he liked having sex with men. That wasn't it. Jesse wouldn't change on the inside. That's where it mattered. I think he couldn't change. I wanted him to see me for who I was. A woman, yes. A woman and not a room. I didn't care that he also loved Metro and loved many other men. I thought I was special because I was the only woman he ever had. I thought I could show him places he never knew existed. Secretly, I wished he would stay there. He did care for a while. And we were close for a while. But Jesse still didn't know who I was. And he didn't know Metro. When I found that out, seeing how fixed Jesse was and fighting some invisible enemy inside him there in the warehouse, I knew it had to be over between us just like it probably had to be over between him and Metro. Only Metro had no place to go. For me, it was like a twig snapping in the woods, some leaf finally crumbling after it had dried out completely. Jesse and I didn't have sex after that. We were friends, suddenly, not lovers. Almost brother and sister. I loved Jesse like I loved Phillip. And I was scared to death for both of them.

That was why I let Phillip stay with me as soon as he was out on parole. We all went places together: Abdul, Phillip, and me. We walked everywhere, even in the chilly evenings, careful to avoid subways and dark streets. We were on the outside now. I heard the wind in my short, bristly hair and in the leafy hands of trees making noise like applause or laughter. Besides, it was springtime. It was time to laugh.

Phillip asked me about Jesse and I said that we were still friends. He asked about my dancing and I took him to the rehearsals. He liked the music most of all. Ellington, Coltrane, even the classical stuff by Stravinsky. "We dance to all music," I told him. "And we do all kinds of dances." I told both of them about Jesse's dance when we had gone to an African restaurant for dinner. When we got back to my place, Phillip and Abdul looked at each other like something was going on between them. Then, to my surprise, Phillip pulled a bottle of champagne from the refrigerator.

"What's the occasion?" I asked.

"Your first professional performance," said Phillip.

"Aw, I perform all the time."

"But you now have a stage to dance on," said Abdul. "And people to watch you."

We started joking then and drank more champagne until we couldn't stop laughing, just the three of us, laughing at nothing much at all. Then Phillip excused himself for bed. That was odd. And early, too. Abdul stayed to talk some more. Something else was fishy, I thought. Like another signal understood by everyone but me. By this time Abdul and I were sitting on the couch. We had another glassful. I tried to keep from noticing how really handsome he was, how strong his hands were, holding mine.

He asked if he could be my boyfriend.

I said nothing. Then I smiled. "You got to promise that I can keep on dancing," I said.

Abdul watched me carefully, too carefully. I couldn't

get enough of his eyes. "You got to promise you're never going to stop." He grinned, showing all his teeth. I closed his lips with mine and didn't even think about taking another breath.

The next night was opening night. I wasn't nervous one bit. Truth is, I wasn't dancing solo any more.

Jesse

I tried to tell Rooms about the dance and the Ellington music I was working with. She kept telling me to call her Ruella, her right name, as if I didn't know it or couldn't let it go. I wanted to tell her about fast travel underground, about taking the A train. She said she'd been there before as Ruella, not Rooms. I had to remember to call her that. So I stopped talking about the A train and told her she was wrong thinking about me and Metro that way. It wasn't like that between us at all. Then what was it?

My dance was about the A train, how close it ran between darkness and light. It wasn't about Metro dying or wanting to die at all. And it wasn't, as she said, about the only kind of travel I knew.

The A train got me to dance class in the first place. It ran along Eighth Avenue and all the way to Harlem and beyond. Once, riding with Metro, we missed the stop at 59th Street and realized our error too late. The next stop wasn't until 125th Street. Harlem. The car shuttled nonstop on uneven tracks until it finally screeched into the station where Metro was an instant foreigner. I was cautious, more cautious than I had to be. I was still new to New York, and I thought about all the rumors I'd heard about Harlem more as a deadly place than the home it actually was for thousands of people as black as me. With Metro, I was afraid. People watched us suspiciously. They were wondering, perhaps, who I was with this frail man with glasses looking curious and lost. I tried to find the platform for the downtown train, and Metro kept staring at the people around us.

"So this is Harlem," he said.

"Harlem," I said. "We won't see much of anything except this station."

"Have you ever seen so many blacks?"

"Of course, Metro. You forget where I come from."

"Yes, sometimes I forget."

"You never get out of the Village. Except to work in midtown."

"Is it dangerous? I mean, here?"

"No more than any other part of the city."

"It reminds me of Baton Rouge on a Saturday night. New Orleans, too, but rougher."

"You're exaggerating, Metro. Come on, let's get to the other side for the downtown train."

"Wait a minute. Let's explore a little."

"Some other time."

"What are you so apprehensive about? What do you have to be afraid of?"

"I'm thinking about you, that's all."

"I'm all right. I can take care of myself. Why are you so nervous?"

"I'm not nervous."

"Well, let's get out of the station and walk the streets or something."

"Some other time. I'm not ready. Besides, I have things to do downtown."

"You always have things to do."

Then we heard the train and saw its lights bearing into the station. We ran up the stairs, across the passageway above, and down the other side. I held the door open. Metro got in reluctantly. He didn't say anything.

"We'll stay longer next time," I said.

"You mean when we make another mistake?"

"I really mean it, Metro. I'm in a hurry this time."

"I'll go on my own," he said, looking from the window and into the glare of stations passing by. "Besides, I need to know more about the city. For my job." Then he was quiet for the rest of the rattling ride downtown. The silence between us made the trip seem longer than it was. We got out of the train at Columbus Circle.

"I don't see what you're so ashamed of," Metro said. "You didn't grow up there."

"No, I didn't," I said. "But someplace just as bad."

"Bad? What's so bad about it?"

"Look, don't try to tell me how to be black." I said nothing more.

Metro made it to Harlem before I had a chance to go with him. He knew someone at work who had a place there. But Metro made it to Harlem by himself. He was in a hurry; he was anxious, as if there was something waiting for him there. But it had nothing to do with me. Nothing. Not even if Albany Avenue in Hartford had just as many fried-chicken stands and storefront churches as 125th Street. I knew where I came from, and I didn't need any guilt-ridden white boy who had been to France telling me how to live. Or Ruella telling me which spaces to occupy. What did Metro know about hugging the rusting radiator for heat in our apartment, or finding our kitchen plumbing clogged with roach shit, or how my college dorm room and scholarship had already been paid for by all the summer jobs I could have had if I had been white, or by all the rent increases we were charged for the same four-room apartment where Charlie and I heard our parents screwing in the next room, or by my traveling south with my mother on a train steaming somewhere in South Carolina where I couldn't pee until we found the Colored Toilet back in 1957? What did Metro know about that? What did he care when all he wanted to do was to call me a nigger to my face and say it was love talking that way, that excitement and abuse went together in sexual pleasure like cock and mouth or cock and ass or black and white when he was fucking not me but the image of me and black men like me that he had always dreamed about as he sat on his Louisiana gallery swatting mosquitoes and dragonflies.

Which is what I tried to tell Ruella: I was calling Metro just what he was—although I hadn't even been that far underground when I met him or followed the stare from his angular face, which became a ladder out of the occupied classroom at Wesman straight into his waiting hands. Hands that held mine tentatively on a walk through the campus at midnight or led me away from the dance stage in Manhattan to some filthy abandoned warehouse where the single word "nigger" had already sealed his fate and was about to seal mine.

I took a crosstown cab that afternoon. I was already late for dance class. Then I saw Ruella. She was pretty. And I knew right away through the dance of our black skins that if I didn't feel her full beauty, I'd never know my own. I thought about my mother. Jessica. Boys named after their mothers are different. But that doesn't give any of us an exclusive right to feel pain, or to hurt others. I tried to say that to Rooms. She made me say "Ruella" first. I could let the name go. I wanted to tell Metro, but he made me take the fast train uptown before he would even listen.

I had a chance to choreograph something. And to dance. I decided upon a simple dance for two men. A *pas de deux* to Ellington's music. I watched black men everywhere for movement: in barbershops, on street corners, some reading the *New York Times,* some going in and out of expensive hotels by the front door and some by the service entrance. And I watched myself: my bend of waist while making the bed, washing dishes, stretching on the parquet floor. And I watched Rodney without his knowing it. I saw the oil glisten from his scalp. I heard the thickness in his voice. I caressed his thick thighs that leapt more powerfully than mine. I fluttered after the gleam from his fingernails as his arms commanded and decorated every space he entered. I saw his grace, his sureness and poise of movement. I wanted to celebrate us—all of us black men. I watched black Wall Street executives leaping from taxis and the man selling subway tokens near our block. I watched the kids playing handball against the supermarket wall and under the sign reading "No Ball Playing." I watched black boys dribbling imaginary basketballs while waiting to take the subway to the next playground. And some balancing real basketballs while riding in the car. I watched white men and black men and short men and fat men and men who were interested in my watching them and others who were not. I wanted to contain them all: men who had come to New York from everywhere else to crowd subways or just go about their regular business of living. And I thought of poor Lonny and how he didn't even know what he was doing. He didn't get anything out of attacking Metro. A couple of weeks in jail, maybe. Some months, maybe a year away at reform school. What else? He was now just a shadow moving across the stage at City Center. He was in the dance, too. A menacing steady presence, a reminder like the ordinary rope that can change in a second to a lyncher's noose or a rescue line out of some dark, endless hole. A reminder that if the business of living was costly in this city of windows and metal gates, the practice of loving could be deadly.

I asked Rodney if he'd help with the dance by practicing some of the trial combinations with me. At first he was reluctant because his ankle was still weak. He blamed the accident at rehearsal on Ruella, but I said it really wasn't her fault. "That woman kept looking at you," he said. "And I was looking at you. How could anyone concentrate with all that looking going on?"

Getting Rodney together with her later didn't help much. He was silent and withdrawn. Later, he admitted being jealous, but only for an instant. And it was that very instant when he lost balance and control and twisted his whole foot. Lucky for him he had only a sprained ankle. We spent more time together back at West 4th Street. We exercised together and attended different dance classes so we could compare notes in the evening as we also compared the angle and depth of our own turn-outs, contractions, leaps, and stretches on the floor as we pulled from equal weight. But when I got the chance to choreograph to Ellington's "A Train," I thought only about Metro and what we shared. I told Rodney about my ideas. He lost interest in working with me.

"No wonder I had trouble with those combinations," he said.

"Was it your ankle?"

"No, Jesse. Those weren't my steps at all. They belonged to someone else."

"How can you tell that? I'm not sure myself and I'm the choreographer."

"By the way the knees bend. I can't get that low. Don't want to, either. I'm into leaps. I'm training for height and speed."

"These steps aren't fast enough? They're closer to a tap dance than modern dance."

"That's just it. They're fast all right. But they're going the other way. Not where I'm headed."

"I see. I'm sorry. I won't ask you again."

"No offense, Jesse. It'll be a fine dance. But when you choose your dancers, try to work with them. Use steps they're comfortable with. Give them a chance to express themselves, too. Isn't that what dance is all about?"

"You're right, Rodney. You're absolutely right."

I tugged at his hair, smoothed the oil on my lips.

I chose the dancers: one white, one black. We practiced after the general rehearsals and often stayed later than anyone else. The dancers liked the music: the grace and deliberate speed of it, the opportunity for improvisation in the rhythm, the solo and personal statement. We were off together improvising on the rush of travel as if we were the instruments and Ellington the conductor/choreographer. But we started playing a different tune than the one I heard riding the A train to Harlem. Even in the harmony of our fast travel underground and aboveground we added leaps and double turns, for we were enjoying the ride, and we were going someplace else. We danced toward the flashing lights all through the tunnel, right on through the real moving rooms that held back the dark.

Lonny 7

Outside the coffee shop the guy looked scared, like I was going to rob him or hit him or scream bloody murder. Then I smiled and he came up to me, still cautious like.

"How old are you?" he asked.

"Fifteen."

"I could get arrested for this. You're a minor."

"Doing what? We ain't doing nothing."

"I got a room nearby. In a hotel."

"Doing what?" I asked him. He looked away from me and into the street like he was expecting something else to happen.

"The ten dollars I gave you," he said.

"Doing what?"

"I can't tell you here."

I didn't do anything but follow him around the block and up a flight of stairs. I just laid on the bed with all my clothes on. I didn't move a muscle.

"I won't hurt you," he said.

I said nothing. I fingered the ten-dollar bill in my pocket.

"What do you want?"

"Make it hard for me. Can you do that?" he said.

"I'm too nervous."

"Take your time. I won't hurt you. I just want to look at it. I won't even touch you."

"Sure? You sure about that?"

"Sure."

I eased my cock out of my pants and didn't have to think about nothing else. I could smell the green money on my hands. It was a long time before I could even jerk myself off without pulling at the new stitches at the end of my balls. Now everything had healed. I made myself hard quick.

"You watching me?" I asked.

"Yeah. It's beautiful. A beautiful cock."

"You watching me?" I said, not moving my eyes from his twisting face.

"Beautiful. Beautiful," he said, wiping the stains seeping into his pants.

I didn't come at all. I couldn't. After a moment my cock went soft. I put it back inside my pants and left. He didn't even know that I was gone.

It was as easy as that.

The very next night I was back again. Same street, same corner. The same man was waiting for me. We went to the same hotel, the same room. It was just like nothing had changed.

"Make it hard for me."

I made it hard.

"Beautiful. Beautiful," he said. His mouth opened and closed. He made funny noises in his throat.

"Can I suck it?"

"Five more dollars," I said, quicker than I really knew what I was saying and surprised I even thought it up so soon.

"All right. Here," he said, throwing the extra bill at me. I pulled my pants down further. He put his mouth to work, and it felt good. Real good.

"Wait a minute," he said.

"You ain't getting your money back," I said. "And you ain't climbing on top, neither."

"I just want to take my teeth out."

Shit, man. Ecstasy! An easy ride to the throat. I should have paid him.

It was another two weeks before I could get back to the

city. I didn't see the man but had no trouble finding another. And another. And another. It got to be a habit. Moms never asked where the extra money was coming from. She got better. And I was cool back at the reform school, so they kept their promise to let me end my bid sooner since Moms was still sick and I was only an accomplice in the crime in the first place. By the time I got out, I had learned to do more with my body—every part of it—and I made more money, too. I had my own corner and didn't have to go into the bars to buy drinks or wink at fat old men. I didn't have to dance like some of the real faggots do in cut-off jeans or satin gym shorts too tight in the crotch. I didn't have to do nothing much at all. Nobody knew my name and nobody cared. I was all face and body. Seems like I didn't even have a name and didn't want or need one. But just for kicks I tried calling myself Starlight and Mister Magic, not anything that would say something about me or what I did. Nothing that could get me back in jail. Then when it was warmer and spring, I wore only jeans and a light jacket. No underwear. The days were longer. Nights warmer. But one night, the magic stopped and for one goddamn scary moment I thought I was through.

"Aren't you Lonny? Lonny Russo?"

I even stopped breathing for a second. Shit.

A woman's voice. A black woman's voice. Someone I didn't even know. A face I didn't remember. A real woman, too, not one of the drag queens who worked the block. This one had real tits and a round ass. Two men were with her. Pimps? Shit, I was scared. I tried being cool.

"Aren't you Lonny?" she said again.

"Naw," I said. "I don't know who you talking about."

"Yes, you are. You remember Jesse, don't you? I'm his friend."

"I don't know nobody like that."

"Remember Metro?"

"Who?"

"Metro. The boy they stabbed in the Village last year?"

"Don't know what you talking about."

She stayed there a moment, not crossing the street. I held my breath. But she kept looking at me like she had my case. Shit. I didn't even know who she was.

"Come on, Ruella," one of the guys said, pulling her across the street.

"We don't want to be late for the program," said the other one.

"But that's Lonny," she said. "I'm sure of it."

"Come on, Ruella. City Center's not too far. We're going to be late."

The black guys also looked at me like they knew who I was. But they kept moving away. I heard one say something to the other, but the woman kept looking back at me like she couldn't believe what she saw. I didn't give a fuck. I didn't have that name anymore. I was Starlight. I was Mister Magic. But the men kept talking. I don't think she heard what they said.

"He's not even pretty."

"But he's young. He can pretend he don't know nothing."

"Yeah. He can say each time is his first."

I felt for the money in my pocket, glad they didn't try anything funny. Then I heard them laughing. Shit. Niggers. Shit. I'm pretty enough, I said to myself. You bet your ass I am. And this pretty sweet ass costs money. Real money. Shit. I left my corner to look for a mirror. I finally found one in the windows of a men's clothing store. I saw my reflection above a pinstriped suit and Italian loafers. There I was: Mister Magic, Mister Starlight himself. Who the fuck did those guys think they was? Who was they talking about? Not me, baby, 'cause this was magic and money, green leaves on a thick tree between my legs, hands touching me and passing green leaves with numbers on them. Who the fuck did they think they was, saying shit like that? Who the fuck did they think I was?

Whenn we finally found our seats I told Phillip and Abdul that it was really Lonny out there in the streets. "So what," Phillip said. "Tell me about this dance. You sure this is going to be good?"

"Yes, Phillip. You saw my program last night. Now you'll see a different one. Jesse's dance comes right after intermission."

"Your sister really danced her heart out last night," said Abdul. I held his hand tighter.

"Glad you both liked it."

"I'd like it even better if you keep on dancing," he said.

"Just the encouragement I need."

"You sure this is going to be good?"

"Just relax, Phillip. Look at all the people here. You'll like Jesse's dance. He's good."

"You ever tell Jesse about what happened to that kid in prison?"

"The one we just saw? Lonny?" I asked. "You want me to tell him what your pals did?"

"Yeah, Junior and Pete and the rest of them got a nut," Phillip said, almost laughing. "We just kept a lookout for the guards."

"Isn't that just as bad?"

"Naw it ain't, Lady. Now don't be mad."

"Ruella."

"All right, *Ruella*. You know me and Abdul ain't into that faggot stuff."

"Shhhh. The lights are dimming."

"That's right, Ruella. Phillip and me ain't into that shit."

"Shhhh. It's about to begin."

"You sure this is going to be good?"

"Shhhh."

"You gonna tell Jesse what happened?"

"Maybe tomorrow I'll tell him. Right now, let's watch that pretty black boy's dance."

Lonny

Y o, man."

"It's Clementine, darling."

"You with the lipstick."

"Indubitably."

"Get the fuck away from here. This is my corner."

"I know. Tonight, I'm buying. Do you speak Italian or French?"

Shit. Just let anybody try to mess with me now.

Jesse

The house lights dimmed. The audience settled back into place. In the darkness I remembered what I had said to Rodney: "Things will be different now between us. I know these aren't your steps. These are Metro's steps. This dance is for him. You are Rodney, black and lovely. I am Jesse. Let's be that to one another. It's already quite a lot." Rodney smiled and turned down the lights. I kissed his darkness and our dance went back and forth, step-leap-and-down. We danced to quiet music and to the applause of our own skin. There were no splinters in his coarse hair or in mine.

A murmur lifted from the stage. The curtain drew up like a big woman gathering her skirts. From my post in the wings, I imagined the first glimmer of light on the dark stage as a beacon from somewhere high revealing a room with an immense fourth wall. From the light came a sudden darkness, then blue, and two fluttering bodies in a dance.

The dancers moved and my body moved with them. Suddenly Metro came alive between the steps: *freight train, caroom-boom-clack.* Their sweat glistening was my sweat streaming out. Their muscles in a voice of trains moved with mine. *And his, and his, my underground man.*

I climbed the warehouse stairs two at a time. I was dressed as Metro would want. Two poppers waited inside my pocket. Our tickets to another time, another room.

"Jesse? Jesse? That you?"

It was early afternoon. The river smelled ripe and blue. The wood of the warehouse floor was soft and slimy on my feet. Nothing here except the shadows and the orange glow of cigarettes here, there, over there. Metro approached unsteadily, his eyes half-open, his underwear sagging from the waist. The smell of medicine seeped from him. River water gurgled and popped from the distant, swaying piles.

Male hands on a male waist. Wheels of legs spinning, leaping. Tiny runs ending in arabesque. Turn–two–three, plié–two–three. Relevé. Arms circling overhead. A reach for air. The bodies swallowed, one into the other.

I held him by the shoulders. No hug, no caress. I simply held him. He knelt on his own. His eyes commanded me. "Push harder," he said. "Push." His head hung lazily to one side. "My head aches. Maybe I've taken too many pills."

"We can try it another way, baby." My voice pleaded with him. I didn't know what to do.

"I need it now. Give me your hands." And he covered his face with my hands, breathing them in.

A second round of rapid runs in a circle of one man's pain. Trains on distant tracks from the music. Hands from one dancer holding the other, lifting and drawing me nearer. In watching them, I was dancing, too, dancing until sweat covered the floor like a cascade of tears now glowing in swirls of radiant, colored stagelights. Then feet reaching for the ground.

Splinters. Watch out for the splinters.

Once he had shaken the tobacco-stained hands of a sharecropper's boy, the son of his mother's maid. And he rode all the way home smelling his hand and knowing how hungry he suddenly was for the rough love they held. The first night we spent together, all he wanted to do was sleep with his nose pressed to the part in my hair. He said my smell came from the soil.

The lights faded from blue to orange. The dancers gained shadow and space. Each threw a bit of his body into the light, captured color and grace from the bare stage.

He fumbled at my jeans. His fingers couldn't hold. "Just take me," he whined. "Give me what you are."

"I don't know what you're talking about Metro." He was shaking in my arms.

"I won't call you nigger ever again. I'll be your nigger. I'm not a white motherfucker. I'm not."

"Who called you that?"

"They did. Out there. In here. What's the difference?"

"Talk sense, Metro. What's gotten into you?"

"I'm not Metro anymore. I'm Uncle Ben, Aunt Jemima."

"And what does that make me, huh? Another nigger, huh."
And before I realized it I was shaking him, slapping him, knocking him about the head. He started to cry. I felt his mouth curl up, the tears cascade. I licked them dry. I held him in my arms. "You don't need it like this, baby. Not like this."

Then saxophone. A flurry of trumpets. Staccato piano. The A-train stride. Arms vibrating, legs twisting. Torsos lean. Feet firm on the ground. Hips whirling in a storm. Floorwork. Wideman extension. Arms reaching up-two-three, curve-two-three, down.

"Hold me," he said, pressing my hands to his chest, making me feel him all over. "Hold me here," he said, guiding my fingers to his throat. "Keep holding. Tight. Tighter. Tighter." His voice was a strained whisper. Air rushed out of him.

Palms flat, knees bent in geometry. Arabesque. The dancer ran and leapt and landed in the waiting arms of the other. My muscles panted loudly with the dancers, my spine arched up and wide. "Touch me. Hold me," my body said from the distance.

"Get your clothes on. I'm taking you out of here."

"Yes, Jesse."

"You all right, now?"

"Yes, I'm better now."

"You go first. Watch your step. Take my hand."

Outside, the air stung me. Blades of sunlight fell from the sky. Metro led me out of the dark, rotting warehouse. I missed a step and stumbled against him. He reached to block my fall. I held tight.

The fourth wall broke open into a gathering wave of hands clapping. Pools of sweat dotted the stage. The applause showered over me. The dancers stood proud, erect. Then quickly, the fourth wall burst into light, and the room holding us there vanished.